Editor-in-Chief and Founder:
  Lyndon H. LaRouche, Jr.
Editorial Board: *Lyndon H. LaRouche, Jr. , Helga
  Zepp-LaRouche, Robert Ingraham, Tony
  Papert, Gerald Rose, Dennis Small, Jeffrey
  Steinberg, William Wertz*
Co-Editors: *Robert Ingraham, Tony Papert*
Managing Editor: *Nancy Spannaus*
Technology: *Marsha Freeman*
Books: *Katherine Notley*
Ebooks: *Richard Burden*
Graphics: *Alan Yue*
Photos: *Stuart Lewis*
Circulation Manager: *Stanley Ezrol*

INTELLIGENCE DIRECTORS
Counterintelligence: *Jeffrey Steinberg, Michele
  Steinberg*
Economics: *John Hoefle, Marcia Merry Baker,
  Paul Gallagher*
History: *Anton Chaitkin*
Ibero-America: *Dennis Small*
Russia and Eastern Europe: *Rachel Douglas*
United States: *Debra Freeman*

INTERNATIONAL BUREAUS
Bogotá: *Miriam Redondo*
Berlin: *Rainer Apel*
Copenhagen: *Tom Gillesberg*
Houston: *Harley Schlanger*
Lima: *Sara Madueño*
Melbourne: *Robert Barwick*
Mexico City: *Gerardo Castilleja Chávez*
New Delhi: *Ramtanu Maitra*
Paris: *Christine Bierre*
Stockholm: *Ulf Sandmark*
United Nations, N.Y.C.: *Leni Rubinstein*
Washington, D.C.: *William Jones*
Wiesbaden: *Göran Haglund*

ON THE WEB
e-mail: eirns@larouchepub.com
www.larouchepub.com
www.executiveintelligencereview.com
www.larouchepub.com/eiw
Webmaster: *John Sigerson*
Assistant Webmaster: *George Hollis*
Editor, Arabic-language edition: *Hussein Askary*

EIR (ISSN 0273-6314) *is published weekly
(50 issues), by EIR News Service, Inc.,
P.O. Box 17390, Washington, D.C. 20041-0390.
(703) 777-9451 ext. 415*

European Headquarters: E.I.R. GmbH, Postfach
Bahnstrasse 9a, D-65205, Wiesbaden, Germany
Tel: 49-611-73650
Homepage: http://www.eirna.com
e-mail: eirna@eirna.com
Director: Georg Neudecker

Montreal, Canada: 514-461-1557

Denmark: EIR - Danmark, Sankt Knuds Vej 11,
basement left, DK-1903 Frederiksberg, Denmark.
Tel.: +45 35 43 60 40, Fax: +45 35 43 87 57. e-mail:
eirdk@hotmail.com.

Mexico City: EIR, Sor Juana Inés de la Cruz 242-2
Col. Agricultura C.P. 11360
Delegación M. Hidalgo, México D.F.
Tel. (5525) 5318-2301
eirmexico@gmail.com

Postmaster: Send all address changes to *EIR*, P.O.
Box 17390, Washington, D.C. 20041-0390.

Signed articles in *EIR* represent the views of the
authors, and not necessarily those of the Editorial
Board.

British Traitors Watch Out!

EDITORIAL

Obama, the Maidan Führer, vs. Trump? Where Does Europe's Real Interest Lie?

by Helga Zepp-LaRouche, chairwoman of the German political party Civil Rights Movement Solidarity (BüSo)

March 4—A *New York Times* article on March 1 demonstrates why the neoliberal, globalist politicians and media in Europe reacted with such amazing arrogance and shamelessness from the very beginning to the victory of the democratically elected U.S. President! In early Autumn, Obama had already begun to downgrade the intelligence classification of numerous dubious intelligence reports about the alleged manipulation of the American electoral process by Russia—reports partially based on British sources and for which there is absolutely no proof still today. This allowed him to maximize the number of people who had access to these reports. Analogous information was also given to European allies—and obviously to certain media.

That explains the unprecedented arrogance with which these circles—as if by pre-arrangement—were so confident that Trump would not serve his full term in the White House, and that "investigative journalists will now have a lot to do," as the *Tagesschau* put it. "Will Donald Trump be murdered, overthrown in a coup, or only impeached?" wrote the British *Spectator*. The same note was struck by the editor of *Die Zeit*, Josef Joffe, who mused about "murder in the White House" on public broadcaster ARD's Press Club program, and by French radio talk show host Karl Zéro in reviewing different murderous ways by which Trump

could soon depart this life, on his daily program broadcast by French public radio, France Info.

The London *Daily Mail* cited an unnamed source—allegedly a friend of the family—saying that Obama wants to personally lead a campaign out of his new mansion in the Kalorama section of Washington, with the goal of removing Trump from the White House, whether through impeachment or resignation.

The Democratic Party repeats, mantra-like, its "narrative" that the supposed Russian hack-attacks were responsible for its defeat, instead of facing the fact that the catastrophic policies of Obama and Hillary Clinton toward "the deplorables" were the cause. Intelligence officials left over from Obama's administration almost daily leak new wiretap recordings to the media, which are supposed to prove inappropriate relations between members of the Trump Administration and Russia. The latest example: conversations that Attorney General Jeff Sessions had with Russian Ambassador to the United States Sergey Kislyak as member of the Senate Armed Services Committee—talks that were a part of his job—are being used by the Democrats as further ammunition to demand Sessions' resignation.

Russian Foreign Minister Sergey Lavrov commented on the charges by "unnamed sources" that Kislyak was a spy and recruiter of spies, by saying that all of this reminds him of the Joe McCarthy period, and President Trump himself has spoken of it as an absolute witch-hunt against himself and his administration.

In fact, it is a new McCarthyite witch-hunt that the neoliberal Establishment on both sides of the Atlantic is orchestrating. It's because Trump has shelved the entire system of "unipolar world" axioms that the United States has pursued since the beginning of the George W. Bush administration—as President Trump had just made clear in his address to a joint session of Congress on Februaty 28. Trump's argument that one could have rebuilt the U.S. economy two or three times over with the $6 trillion that was spent on the wars in the Middle East, highlights the stark contrast.

The Imminent Financial Threat

But while the neoliberal European Establishment is dropping its democratic mask in an astounding manner and is obviously already speculating about a post-Trump era, it would do better to put its own house in order. The signs of a new, even more dramatic financial crisis than that of 2008, the return of the Greek crisis, the Italian banking crisis, the unpredictable outcomes of elections in many countries this year in which one or more countries might follow the Brexit example—the combination of all of these developments could very quickly call into question the very existence of the euro, and of the EU itself. But the EU governments are obviously just as unable or unwilling to abandon the policies that generated these crises, as the Democratic Party in the United States is, to accept the reasons for its defeat.

Five years after the famous statement of Mario Draghi, head of the European Central Bank (ECB), that he will do "whatever is necessary" to save the euro, the euro crisis is back in full force; but the central banks, with their quantitative easing and negative interest rates, have already shot their wad. The austerity policy of the Troika—the European Commission, ECB, and the IMF—toward Greece has ruined its economy and brought unspeakable suffering to the population. The stubborn refusal of German Finance Minister Wolfgang Schäuble to give Greece debt relief and the increasing desperation of the people of Italy, Spain, and Portugal—threaten to trigger the collapse of the global financial system. The Chinese daily, *Global Times*, which is close to the government, has warned of precisely that, and of its ramifications for China.

The Greek crisis is of course only one of many landmines that could detonate the trans-Atlantic financial system. In view of the 3.7 trillion euros that the ECB has frittered away over the last five years for the bankrupt European banking system, and of the U.S. government debt of $20 trillion, everything—not just Trump's future—depends upon him fulfilling his election promise to reintroduce Glass-Steagall and thereby put an end the casino economy.

Banking separation—exactly as FDR carried it out in 1933—is only the first, indispensable step, which must be followed by the other three laws that, as a comprehensive, four-part package, Lyndon LaRouche has defined as necessary to overcome the crisis. The current monetarist policy must be replaced with a return to the American System of Economy in the tradition of Alexander Hamilton, the creation of a national bank and a credit system, and a massive upgrading of the productivity of industry, which can only be achieved with a crash program to develop thermonuclear fusion and international cooperation in space exploration. Resolutions to this effect have already been introduced into 11 state legislatures in the United States.

Even though one may not endorse the view of economics professor Mark Blyth, who thinks the EU could disintegrate in light of the upcoming electoral results in several countries—even before Great Britain activates Article 50 for the Brexit—it should be clear that a "keep it up" policy for the EU and the euro cannot function. Not surprisingly, European Commission President Jean-Claude Juncker offers nothing new in his White Book for solving the European crisis; his five scenarios are only variants of the same neoliberal geopolitical concepts.

The Alternative: Jump Aboard!

The alternative is as clear as day: The European nations must take up China's offer of cooperation with the New Silk Road, called the Belt and Road Initiative. Over the last three years, this project has already totally changed the world dynamic: It has brought 70 nations into collaboration with China in the greatest infrastructure and development program in the history of mankind. Instead of trying to strike extremely dubious deals with Mediterranean countries, Mrs. Merkel should rather seize China's offers to build up, along with other countries, the Middle East and the African continent, and thus to solve the refugee crisis permanently, and in a human fashion.

Apparently the blockheads of neoliberal politics are unable to do this. Finance Minister Schäuble insists on a pound of flesh; he will not even consider debt relief for Greece. China is not only expanding the port of Piraeus as a terminal for the New Silk Road, but is investing in upgrading the rail link from Athens through Belgrade to Budapest, to make it high-speed rail. And what is the EU Commission doing? It is trying to block this project!

It is high time that more and more people join with the BüSo in mobilizing for the true interests of Germany and the other European nations, which lie in cooperation with China, Russia, India, Japan, and other countries on this grand perspective which the New Silk Road has put on the agenda. It is absolutely not in our interest to participate in the witch-hunt against Trump or Putin, and we should be delighted that the new American President rejects wars of intervention.

We have to consider, above all, why large parts of the world find themselves in such a chaotic situation: The cause is the unipolar policy of Bush, Thatcher, Blair, Obama, and Cameron, including the imperial expansion of NATO and the EU up to the borders of Russia, the policy of regime change through color revolutions and wars in Eastern Europe, as well as in the Middle East and North Africa. That includes the neoliberal economic policy with its priority on the interests of the bankers and speculators, so that the Establishment will do better and better, while not even considering the "deplorables" worthy of being deplored.

As you can see, these neoliberals are perfectly illiberal, not to say dictatorial, when democratic majorities go against them.

Fortunately it is not too late to jump aboard of the train of the New Silk Road!

EIR Contents

www.larouchepub.com Volume 44, Number 10, March 10, 2017

Creative Commons

Cover This Week

The actor Peter Capaldi is shown here for fictional character purposes.

Correction
A picture caption on page 22 of *EIR*, March 3, misidentified Jim Bridenstine as a former Congressman. He is currently a Congressman.

I. Our Goals for Mankind

Trump, Lincoln, And LaRouche's Four Laws

by Robert Ingraham

March 5, 2017—The speech which President Donald Trump delivered to a joint session of Congress on February 28, contained the following remarks:

It's been a long time since we had fair trade. The first Republican President, Abraham Lincoln, warned that the "abandonment of the protective policy by the American government… will produce want and ruin among our people." Lincoln was right—and it's time we heeded his advice and his words…

In nine years, the United States will celebrate the 250th anniversary of our founding—250 years since the day we declared our independence. It will be one of the great milestones in the history of the world. But what will America look like as we reach our 250th year? What kind of country will we leave for our children?

On our 100th anniversary, in 1876, citizens from across our nation came to Philadelphia to celebrate America's centennial. At that celebration, the country's builders and artists and inventors showed off their wonderful creations. Alexander Graham Bell displayed his telephone for the first time. Remington unveiled the first typewriter. An early attempt was made at electric light. Thomas Edison showed an automatic telegraph and an electric pen. Imagine the wonders our country could know in America's 250th year.

Think of the marvels we can achieve if we simply set free the dreams of our people. Cures to the illnesses that have always plagued us are not too much to hope. American footprints on distant worlds are not too big a dream. Millions lifted from welfare to work is not too much to expect. And streets where mothers are safe from fear, schools where children learn in peace, and jobs where Americans prosper and grow are not too much to ask.

When we have all of this, we will have made America greater than ever before—for all Americans. This is our vision. This is our mission. But we can only get there together. We are one people, with one destiny. We all bleed the same blood. We all salute the same great American flag. And we all are made by the same God.

When we fulfill this vision, when we celebrate our 250 years of glorious freedom, we will look back on tonight as when this new chapter of American Greatness began. The time for small thinking is over. The time for trivial fights is behind us. We just need the courage to share the dreams that fill our hearts, the bravery to express the hopes that stir our souls, and the confidence to turn those hopes and those dreams into action…

True love for our people requires us to find common ground, to advance the common good, and to cooperate on behalf of every American child who deserves a much brighter future…

From now on, America will be empowered by our aspirations, not burdened by our fears; inspired by the future, not bound by the failures of the past; and guided by our vision, not blinded by our doubts."

I. The Axiomatic Approach to Moving Forward

How is this vision—so eloquently enunciated by President Trump—to be actualized? What is the pathway we must take if we are to successfully return the United States of America to the "Temple of Hope and

Beacon of Liberty" it must once again become, by its 250th birthday in 2026? The challenge is manifest; the battle-plan, for many, remains unclear.

In 2014, Lyndon LaRouche issued the three page document *The Four New Laws to Save the U.S.A. Now!* That document, whose Four Laws are grounded in the principles of *Public Credit and National Banking*, as promulgated by Alexander Hamilton, remains, starkly, as the only viable solution to the banking and economic crisis facing the United States and the world today. *It defines the only possible strategy for fulfilling President Trump's promise to create a "new chapter of American Greatness"*—and in the process to lay the basis, in cooperation with friendly foreign nations, for the beginning of a new global economic and scientific Renaissance.

The paramount feature of those Four Laws is to be found in the concluding paragraphs of the document. It is here that LaRouche defines the basis for all economic policy. He says,

The knowable measure, in principle, of the difference between man and all among the lower forms of life, is found in what has been usefully regarded as the naturally upward evolution of the human species, in contrast to all other known categories of living species. The standard of measurement of these compared relationships, is that mankind is enabled to evolve upward, and that categorically, by those voluntarily *noëtic* powers of the human individual will.

Mankind's progress, as measured rather simply as a species, is expressed typically in the rising power of the principle of human life, over the abilities of animal life generally, and relatively absolute superiority over the powers of

The White House Historical Association

Grant and Lincoln. Excerpt of the White House copy of the lost 1868 painting. Sherman, Grant, Lincoln, and Porter aboard the River Queen on March 27th & March 28th, 1865.

non-living processes to achieve within mankind's willful intervention to that intended effect. Progress exists so only under a continuing, progressive increase of the productive and related powers of the human species. That progress defines the absolute distinction of the human species from all others presently known to us. A government of people based on a policy of 'zero-population growth and per capita standard of human life' is a moral, and practical abomination.

It is in this section of the Four Laws that LaRouche defines a scientifically precise notion of *human productivity*. LaRouche's words echo the intent of the *Preamble* of the United States Constitution as well as the sentiment expressed in Abraham Lincoln's Gettysburg Address. It is in the *noëtic* creative distinction between members of the human species and all of the lower beasts that proper economic policy must be grounded.

Real economics, economics as LaRouche defines it "as the naturally upward evolution of the human species" is not about money or profits, as those terms are usually understood. Rather, it is the purpose of a Hamiltonian system, anchored by the principles of *Public Credit* and *National Banking*, to establish a sound basis whereby an escalating increase in human and national productivity might be realized.

When the Gouverneur Morris-authored *Preamble* speaks of "We the People...," or when Lincoln speaks of a government "of the people, by the people, and for the people...," the profundity of that idea-content must not be obscured by maudlin romanticism. Rather, it represents an intention—to marshal the power of government to advance the opportunities, skills, talents and productivity of the citizens of the nation, to aid in the emergence of a national culture grounded in happiness.

II. Lincoln and Grant

If one examines the entire sweep of Abraham Lincoln's policy initiatives—from the protectionist tariff policies to the Greenback national credit policy; from the Emancipation Proclamation to the Homestead Act; from the Transcontinental Railroad to the Land-Grant Colleges Act—all of these are aimed at accomplishing a powerful improvement in the *physical economy* of the nation, accompanied by an increase in productivity and opportunity for

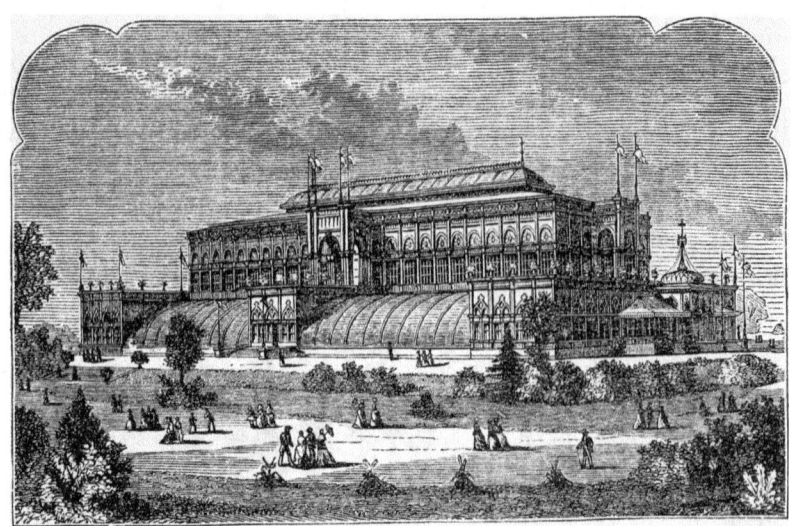

Library of Congress

The Philadelphia Centennial Exposition

the all of the citizenry. Neither *de jure* slavery nor *de facto* economic servitude were to be tolerated. As LaRouche puts it, the outlook was grounded "in the rising power of the principle of human life, over the abilities of animal life generally."

Lincoln launched an economic revolution, and he quickly found himself at war with entrenched monied interests, particularly with leading Wall Street banking houses and the financial institutions of the British Empire's City of London. Their system was a *money system*; his was a *physical economic system*. Beginning in 1861, and continuing over the next four years, the New York Associated Banks, and their leader James Gallatin, relentlessly endeavored to destroy the Lincoln Presidency, demanding that President Lincoln's efforts to impose national sovereignty over economic and banking policy be killed.

The outlook of those 19th century financiers is no different than what we hear today, emanating from Wall Street apologists who denounce *Glass-Steagall* legislation as "government interference" into private banking matters and deleterious to their designs to accumulate speculative financial profits. Lincoln, like Hamilton, comprehended the power and responsibility of government to regulate, and even promulgate, policy related to banking and finance, so as to secure a Credit Policy that achieves the greatest reward for the common good. Such an approach is the only one that honors the Oath of Office to uphold the United States Constitution.

In truth, only those policies—economic or otherwise—which stem from an intention to "establish Justice, insure domestic Tranquility, provide for the

common defence, promote the general Welfare, and secure the Blessings of Liberty to ourselves and our Posterity" can be rightfully considered lawful, either in the strict sense of U.S. Constitutional Law, or from the vantage point of a natural law which recognizes the unique nature of the human species.

It is also within this intention to promote the General Welfare and to secure a positive future for the children of the United States of America, that President Trump's praiseworthy vow to "stop the drugs from pouring into our country and poisoning our youth" must be seen. This is a sacred promise to yet unborn generations, and many nations will be eager to work with the United States in such an effort.

1876: Philadelphia Centennial Exposition

President Trump's extended reference to the 1876 Philadelphia Centennial Exposition is truly heartening. Implied, but unstated in his remarks, is the reality that the industrial and scientific wonders that were there displayed, were all made possible through the intention and effects of the Lincoln Economic Revolution. Also left unsaid in the President's remarks was that the Exposition was organized under the Presidency of Ulysses Grant, who attended the opening ceremony and flipped the switch to turn on the Corliss Steam Engine, then the most powerful engine in the world.

Grant's Presidency was characterized by an ironclad commitment to secure equal rights for Black Americans. It was Grant who initiated military campaigns against the Ku Klux Klan; it was Grant who defended black voting rights with U.S. troops; and it was

Grant who defended and supported the creation of educational institutions for freed slaves. This included his use of troops to defend the facilities of the Freedmen's Bureau, an organization created by Abraham Lincoln; and his later support for the black universities which were being established.

This is the same Grant who, beginning in 1869, put an end to the wars of extermination against American Indians. For Grant, as with Lincoln, celebrating the triumphs of American science and inventiveness was not separate from the commitment to human equality and justice. For Lincoln, economic and financial policies were never allowed to serve the financial elites—every policy, every initiative must have as its intention to "secure the blessings of liberty" to every one of the nation's citizens, as well to secure a better world—a better future—for the nation's posterity.

Today, the policies of Glass-Steagall, national banking, public credit, and a science policy centered on fusion energy and space exploration will—as LaRouche defines in his Four Laws—fulfill exactly that mission, as defined in the Lincoln and Grant Presidencies from 1861 to 1877. A financial system which generates speculative mega-profits, while little is produced in terms of tangible physical wealth, leaving millions to languish in poverty, is not the legacy of our greatest President. A nation's credit is a bounty; it should not be squandered on frivolous things, but put to work building for the future.

III. Partners

Abraham Lincoln stated, in a speech shortly before his 1861 inauguration, that the American Declaration of Independence "gave liberty not alone to the people of this country, but hope to all the world, for all future time."

It should come as no surprise that both Lincoln and Grant approached foreign powers from the standpoint of winning friends based on the Principles embedded in that Declaration. From Lincoln's friendly initiatives with Russia, Japan and Benito Juarez's Mexico, to Grant's world tour of 1877-1879, the United States offered a hand of friendship to every nation in the world, an offer which stemmed from a genuine desire to work with other nations in the great task of uplifting civilization through science, industry and the eradication of human impoverishment.

Today, in 2017, the tables have turned, and it is now the nations of China and Russia, together with their partners, who are offering a helping hand to the United States—to aid the United States in recovering from the 16 years of murderous geopolitics unleashed by George W. Bush and Barack Obama, to join with them in building a great world-wide economic and scientific Renaissance.

The Belt and Road Forum for International Cooperation (BRF) will be held in Beijing from May 14 to 15 of this year. Already, more than 65 countries, encompassing more than half of the human race, have joined this initiative. More than 20 heads of state, including President Xi Jinping of China, President Vladimir Putin of Russia, and President Rodrigo Duterte of the Philippines will be in attendance. This conference is a watershed event in the ongoing work of the Chinese *One Belt-One Road* policy, a policy which is redefining relations among nation states away from imperial geopolitical conflict toward cooperation and major economic development projects.

President Trump should attend the May Conference in Beijing. Were Lincoln and Grant alive today, they would not hesitate. The world today does not need more wars. Great economic projects and great scientific challenges —the type of challenges which pull nations together as partners and friends —is the required future.

Speaking to an audience in New York City on February 4, 2017, Helga Zepp-LaRouche declaimed,

> And I think if we can convince the United States with the Trump administration to cooperate with China on the New Silk Road, I am safe on the prediction that Mr. Trump will not be only a great American President, but if he can mobilize his country to join hands with China right now, he will go into history as one of the towering giants of all of universal history.

The operative word in Mrs. LaRouche's statement is "if." It is a word pregnant with potential, but it is not yet realized. America's 250th birthday is nine years away. As President Trump asked, "But what will America look like as we reach our 250th year? What kind of country will we leave for our children?" The answer is right in front of us. The still-living minds of Abraham Lincoln and Alexander Hamilton, together with the economic principles defined by Lyndon LaRouche in his Four Laws, offer the path that will get us to that promised great future.

The Method for Victory—Fighting for The Highest Conception of Mankind

The following is taken from the transcript of La-Rouche PAC National Activists Call of March 2, 2017.

Dennis Speed: On behalf of the LaRouche Political Action Committee, I want to welcome you to tonight's Fireside Chat, the first one after the State of the Union Address. There have been discussions during the day today between our Policy Committee and Lyn and Helga LaRouche, and we're going to get right into the core of that.

During the State of the Union, one of the things that President Trump emphasized is that in nine years, it will be 2026, the 250th anniversary of the founding of the American Republic, and the question is what will the country look like at that time and what future will our country be projecting from that time. We should think about it this way: What will the country look like 250 years in the future—and ten weeks from today; because ten weeks from today approximately, there is a conference going on in Beijing which Donald Trump needs to be at and he needs to have a certain perspective in going into that conference. To discuss that and the other matters we're going to have Mike Steger take us into that discussion right now.

Michael Steger: We're clearly at a historical period of great, great change or at least the potential for it. There are two things that I want to address, and then I think over the course of the discussion tonight we can dig into more of the implications or aspects that stem from that discussion.

Mr. LaRouche put a very strong emphasis on continuing to integrate and unify the process. There are two aspects to that. One is clearly the question of the American political process at stake today. The idea, and I think this came from Sen. Joe Manchin from West Virginia, who basically described the process in Congress as nearly unbearable; that to even talk to a Republican is basically an act of treason at this point within the Democratic Party Caucus. Now this division is entirely artificial—it's a fraud, it's false, it's imposed. It's imposed by Obama. It's imposed by Obama's controllers—Valerie Jarrett, Soros. It's directly a British oper-

ation to break up what should be the real American political tradition, that you fight for the nation, you operate on the principle of the interest of the country, and not on the party. We have these kind of divisions in the country, and clearly the divisions exist in the minds of the American people, but they don't necessarily exist in the society. There is great unity as Diane Sare and Mr. and Mrs. LaRouche have addressed many times before, there is a clear unity in the American people. Even Robert Reich, the so-called "liberal from Berkeley" went out to Iowa and said, "Wow, these Tea Party guys actually agree on a lot of the same things that the liberals do: Glass-Steagall, going after Wall Street, maintaining Social Security and Medicare." If people go out and talk to the American people, you realize this is the case; 80 to 90 percent of the American people agree on core questions.

But the objective is to unify the process according to the future and that's what we've got to do. With Trump's speech, what he opened up—he increased the potential, because he took an optimistic tone. He captured the tone of Lincoln, of FDR, of Kennedy, in much of what he addressed in the more substantial aspects. That's where you see the real American political tradition.

As many on this call know, Mr. LaRouche has put forward *four new laws,* and we can get more into that in detail; but that is the base by which we pull together a bipartisan caucus inside the political process of the country to move on these policies and this agenda, this infrastructure, the space program, the collaboration with Russian and China—these legislative issues that have to be addressed—we've got to pull this thing together, of course, starting with Glass-Steagall.

The other aspect of it, though,—and this is where we have to take a step back from the immediate kind of melodrama of the American political media, because much of this is just straight political theater for distraction; much of it, though it seems to be targeted toward Russia and the United States, I would say that much of it is also a distraction away from the Wall Street question, which is the Achilles' heel of this entire failed British system. So if we take a step back from this political melodrama, what you see and what we have been very clear on—what was very obvious during the Obama period—is that the interventions by Putin of Russia and by China are right now a substantial aspect of the political process of the United States. They have stabilized much of what could have been chaos and even potentially nuclear war under Obama, and they shifted the discussion drastically. They created very viable alternatives to deal with the terrorism question, to deal with the economic crisis.

I could say more on that, but to keep it pointed here, it is not just Russia and China; there is a shifting process globally and that has to be incorporated, and the actions we take and the interventions we are taking now, have to incorporate this kind of global change that is occurring. Because it really is a global crisis. This financial and economic breakdown is one of global proportions and the actions that are going to be taken to address it, have to be taken both within the United States, but then also in collaboration with many other nations on a global scale. A new global economic system has to be created. As Dennis pointed out, over the coming next two and one-half months, we are going into a summit in Beijing which definitely provides the potential for that.

Michael Vadon

Donald Trump in Laconia, New Hampshire.

A Renaissance of Global Proportions

Now, the other emphasis from the discussion this morning is that this organization must take immediate action: We have been the leadership on these questions for fifty years, the question of a new global economic system, the question of shutting down the drug war and the speculation and the terrorism by going directly after Wall Street; and using that as the basis for then creating the kind of funding for the development of the country—the scientific agenda, the space program, fusion research—and at an even higher level to really unleash, willfully, a new Renaissance for mankind. At this point, not just within the United States and Europe, but what is now possible, is to launch a Renaissance of global proportions. That's what we've got to take as an initiative now.

What Trump has opened up is a potential. It is not a question of "like Trump, don't like Trump." There is clear potential today with Obama pushed off the scene, at least pushed out of power. You've got an opening for the American people to reassert the true intent of our republic. Our republic was shaped to escape the degeneracy, religious wars, and cultural deterioration of Europe, and that idea was launched by the very figures who founded and launched the Renaissance in Italy, and they looked to continue that in the United States. That's what we are resurrecting today. So in nine and one-half years, at that 250th birthday of the founding of our republic, we should be celebrating not only a rebirth, but a birth of something entirely new for mankind, a flourishing of creativity on the planet as a whole for the first time in human history. I think that is really the intrinsic nature of what our country was founded to help initiate as a platform.

Now that means to do this—and to do this now, because the moment is clearly urgent. This is something Mrs. LaRouche clearly emphasized: The one thing we know for sure about Donald Trump is that our enemies, the enemies of mankind, the enemies of our country, are hysterical. That is a clear sign that there is something potential and available to us today, to create what has not been there before. I think their hysteria speaks for itself, as we see today on the whole Russia question reignited.

We are launching this tonight, and we are going to sustain our efforts over the course of this week with an intense level of mobilization. That means we're going to have a new pamphlet, which will be released sometime by early next week, if not earlier. This will be a pamphlet which can be circulated digitally, by email, all possible ways—we'll come up with different ways of distributing this. And obviously, we want to get this thing printed and in physical distribution. But that will be available, and it will have an emphasis on the Four Laws with an emphasis on the fourth and third extensively, as well as the financial and banking aspects; but also a comprehensive overview of both the economic destruction of the United States, and the kind of international developments that have occurred over the last three years to make what is now a global Renaissance so very possible.

It was just last week that General Electric, one of the biggest industrial companies of the United States, was complaining about the lack of credit they had available. So, if you're going to really launch the kind of credit available, to lend and develop the United States, to the small businesses, to the large corporations, to re-industrialize the United States, we've got to move on Glass-Steagall. I think over 2,000 signatures were collected. If people have those, we should continue to turn those in. We want to get back to everyone that signed; we want to get back to them and fold them into this continuing mobilization. This is not an issue orientation: This is a mobilization for victory.

We're going to come out with another petition which will again focus of the Four Laws and help to bring even more people into this political fight. We are also intending to do another Day of Action in Washington. We had a number of good discussions with Republicans on the Hamilton National Bank. We want more meetings to discuss this because if you're going to do the infrastructure, you're going do the space program, you're going to continue to maintain an industrial manufacturing base in the United States, you're going to have to go with this economic program. There's no other way to do it. You can't just print more money, you can't just hack the budget, you can't go with private-public partnerships; you have to go with an entirely new banking system the way that Mr. LaRouche has put forward.

The idea is that there is clearly a unique moment. This past week, the State Councilor of the People's Republic of China met for two days inside the White House and with Secretary of State Tillerson, meeting with all the top advisors to the Trump administration. Clearly the question of U.S.-Russia collaboration is all over the media and our enemies are hysterical about that potential collaboration. And the questions of the devastation of the U.S. economy, as President Trump made very clear in his State of the Union—94 million people out of the labor force not working; 45 million people in poverty, 40-some million people on food

stamps the opioid addiction that's tripled in just the last four or five years in terms of overdoses and deaths.

So, we are at a moment of great crisis, but we are clearly at a moment of great opportunity. The [Italian] Renaissance was launched by a small handful of people, whom you would have described as fairly insignificant. They weren't in high positions of power, and yet had a clear intention to accomplish and achieve something that had never been done before, and to build something that by its awe and magnitude captured the imagination of everyone who saw it and even of those who just simply heard about it: the great Florentine Dome built by Brunelleschi. But, in building a new economic system and a new collaboration of nations today, we can strike a quality of the human mind to create a quality of optimism and development within the human species that is unparalleled in human history. That's what we have the potential to unleash, and it is going to take a very, very focused grouping of people dedicated to launch these kinds of policies now: on the banking question, on Glass-Steagall, but really to fulfill the long-term developments—the fusion program, the space program—and to reignite the productive potential of the American people.

Speed: When Mr. LaRouche began the Manhattan Project a couple of years ago, he emphasized to us that the issue was a "single unified effort by a single nation" and a population which subordinated all forms of confederacy, any form of localism, any form of weirdness (if you want to put it that way), to a single mission. I think the only thing I would say is we're embarked on that mission. We have a Presidency unlike the inhuman one which just vacated the White House, which can be responsive to our initiatives.

I'd like to get one or two reports from the lobbying in Washington.

Intervention in Congress

Question: This is Alvin in New York. So, first, in two particular meetings, where we had ten activists, the staffers were given very brief but very comprehensive presentations on Glass-Steagall, the Four Laws, the New Paradigm, Russia, China, the Ukraine dossier, and the attacks on Trump/the color revolution. These were discussed not as single or separate subjects, but that required an understanding in their relationship to one another and the action that then must be taken. Typically, for me, in the trips I've been making down there, that's the end of the meeting, perhaps a couple of questions, we leave a stack of literature, and then the meeting's over.

But—you're talking about LaRouche calling for a unifying process—and for the first time that concept became real to me, because [New York City choral director and organizer] John Sigerson came down with us, and introduced himself at various points, and began to go through the cultural program of Mr. LaRouche and what he is in charge of, here in the United States: the generation of our citizens and how this type of culture around Mozart and beauty was really the only way to have a real victory and turn the nation around. And in each case, he handed both of these staff members the DVD of the *Requiem* concert for the memorial for JFK in Boston.

It really wasn't until the trip back that I began to realize what had gone on there, and this was a completely different dynamic from anything I'd ever experienced. I could only appreciate it on the ride back. Common sense would say that at the point where we finish the things we had to say, the meeting would be over, as it had been in the past, but this took the thing to another level. Their plates were full already, and then John comes by and lays this on them.

So to me, on the ride back, I laughed and said, "Lyndon LaRouche is really outrageous! And what we did today was outrageous and it was a lot of fun!" Who knows how they'll process all of this, but it was, again, just that type of unifying process that John has been working with us on.

John Sigerson: What Alvin said is absolutely right. One of the reasons why I intervened in the way I did was that I simply sat down the other day and re-read LaRouche's original piece called, "The Four New Laws To Save The U.S.A. Now! Not an Option: An Immediate Necessity." And really what struck me—we have this as a handout now; the first page is all about the Four Laws, but then, there's a topic which is called "Vernadsky on Man and Creation" and then another topic called "Chemistry: The Yardstick of History."

The Highest Conception of Mankind

And I looked at this and said to myself, "Well, this is really interesting, because I'm sure that some people will read this first page, and say, 'Oh, that's it. And then, there's all this gobbledygook about Vernadsky and about Kepler and so forth. And I don't understand all this stuff, but I guess he just put in there to fill up the page, or something like that.'" But, knowing LaRouche as long as I have, I know the reason why he put this in, is specifically because he wants to indicate to people where he's coming from. Because in all of these cases, he's really coming from the highest conception of mankind. This paragraph really sort of blew my mind, when he says here that—I mean, here, we're talking about the Four Laws, and he's starting to talk about the fact that space and time are merely useful images, and therefore, you cannot say that "space" and "time" actually exist as a set of "metrical principles of the Solar System."

What?! I mean, c'mon! But then he says,

"The essential characteristic of the human species, is its distinction from all other species of living processes: a principle which is, scientifically, rooted for all competent modern science on the foundations of the principles set forth by Filippo Brunelleschi (the ontological minimum),"

—What?!

Members of the LaRouche PAC "basement team" discuss LaRouche's ideas on science.

—"Nicholas of Cusa," the discovery of "the ontological maximum"

—*What?!*

"and the positive discovery by mankind by Johannes Kepler, of a principle coincident with the perfected Classical human singing scale" adopted by Kepler "and elementary measure of the Solar System within the still larger universe of the Galaxy, and higher orders in the universe."

Well! Well!

And this sort of reminds one of the kinds of classes that Lyndon LaRouche used to give, where he would always start with at least 2,000 years of history—usually many more than that. In other words, he always attempted to completely expand people's conception of what they themselves are thinking and doing. And so, that to me is so important, and I think that the more people who do that, that is, that you have to say—well, first of all you have to say to yourself, "where am I coming from?" Am I simply coming from a sense of activism and anger and so forth? Am I actually coming from exactly this idea of mankind? Is that really my motivation? Or is it simply icing on the cake of whatever I think that I am doing. And I think everybody on the call should maybe go back and re-read this, but just think about that, in terms of—because the clearer you are about where you're coming from, the better a leader you're going to be. And that's what we need, is more leaders.

Steger: Just to follow up what John said, LaRouche today towards the end of the discussion came back to that specific point: You've got to make it about mankind. It's got to be a question of mankind. Because we're calling on principles for human development; we're not calling on things that maybe seem appropriate based on immediate circumstances—that maybe this we can stitch things together and solve the problems. We're calling upon universal principles and acting upon those which are uniquely accessible to the human mind to address this problem, not just for our nation, but for mankind as a whole.

And so, Lyn echoed very much John's sentiments from the Four Laws again today, and I think he probably has for the last fifty ears.

Question: K____ from Seattle asks how we could pressure Trump to push Glass Steagall.

Steger: I appreciate your Question, it's important to bring this back up. There are two aspects to this question, and it gets to the heart of what John, and Dennis and Alvin were raising right now.

[Steger here delineates the various interventions people can do with elected officials and institutions, then proceeds to the issue of principle.]

How to Think

Then we get to the other Question, which is, *how do we think about it?* And I think this is where, oftentimes, every other political organization or movement runs into a problem, because without access to a sense of what creativity is, as a process, you lack to the ability to think, "well, wait a minute, we can do all these things, we can be very busy about this. How do you transcend a boundary? If you have a system in place, as we do today, that is fundamentally opposed to a policy like Glass-Steagall, because Glass-Steagall does not mean you're adding on to the system; you are ending this system, you are transforming it. So there is a *huge* amount of resistance. There are other things you can compare it to, but you get this sense, there is a tremendous amount of political resistance to this.

As you said, President Trump committed to this in his campaign, and he's re-verified that at certain points since he's been elected. But how do we overcome this political resistance? And this is where, I think, what Mr. LaRouche laid out today, people have to have a sense of this—the American people; I talked to a couple of people today, someone from China, and she remarked that the American people are very parochial, which is very true! Now in some cases that's good. Many of these people are the people backing Trump because they have their fifth, or sixth, or seventh generation American, and they have a sense of what this country's been over the last century and a half. But there's another problem, which is that they don't know what's happening in the world. And we are a leading nation in the world! Our economy is integrated into the world, and what's taking place politically in major countries, especially in Asia, increasingly in Europe, is becoming a kind of political shift towards a new system, a new paradigm for development.

Willful Evolution

And this is something that takes people to a higher principled level, it gives them access to recognize that mankind as a whole is willfully deciding to evolve, to break out of the shackles of this monetary system, of so-called "cheap labor" policies, or just extraction of natural resources. Mankind is now beginning to look at its unique potential: to develop our planet, to develop our species, and to develop the human population, and that's the most important characteristic.

China's been leading this, with a policy they call the *Belt and Road*. Russia has been directly involved in collaboration on that. India is fighting its own political questions, but they're getting involved. And there's an increasing number of nations in Africa, Central Asia, even in South America and Europe, who are joining this kind of orientation. And China is going to be holding a summit on May 14-15, with heads of state and government on this project of development.

So that's a significant question. And many Americans just don't have a sense—this project is eleven times the size of the Marshall Plan—and it's potentially much bigger. It involves over 4.5 billion people. We've gone through these numbers, but for those who haven't heard them, they're somewhat shocking.

And this is only one aspect, because, what John Sigerson just raised is, why does mankind have the ability to do this? Why do we have this voluntary ability to transform our environment, to think about three or four generations ahead of us, and to begin to initiate projects today that will ultimately be fulfilled by those generations, like the space program?

So, there are certain things that, when you engage in a discussion with someone, whether it be your congressman, your state representative, a speaker at a university, or your sister, or your son, or your parents, or your neighbor—how do you engage people to get outside the discussion which oftentimes is a very limited environment; how do we get Trump and Congress to, say, pass Glass-Steagall? That's what we want as an effect, but when you put it in that confined context, it almost seems like Zeno's paradox—the closer you get, the farther away it becomes.

So you have to say, well, how do we change that quality of discussion? And oftentimes, it's by getting people to recognize there's something much bigger taking place on this planet; there's something much more profound about humanity than the problems we're addressing right now. And we've got to situate people in that kind of discussion, and once we do, all of a sudden you see a light go on in someone's mind. You start to see them get more optimistic; you start to see them talk about things you never heard them say before. They end up more engaged in the process emotionally, and there's now a shift. There's now a more potential human being ready to do something.

Self-Activating Outreach

And Mr. LaRouche said this today: our outreach has to be something which is self-activating. We have to bring people who will begin to activate themselves and then begin to provoke others to then also activate themselves. It can't be something like we're going to marshal people out of anger. It's got to be a sense of what we're capable of accomplishing as human beings.

And so I think how we approach that, these quality of ideas—and if you go back, we've been re-publishing Mr. LaRouche's papers in *EIR* magazine; if you go back and look at any one of these, you get a sense that this is what Mr. LaRouche has been developing as a science for over 50 years—this question of how do you self-activate a creative process, within an individual, but also within a social process? And how do you then take advantage, or how do you employ that creativity toward a higher end for mankind? How do you turn it into a political process? And more and more of that kind of discussion is the substance of it.

We have to mobilize people now from the highest standpoint to move, because clearly just based on the reaction of our enemy, the time is of great urgency. We have a moment to bring Glass-Steagall to bear, that is very clear. There is a bipartisan effort in Congress; there is massive bipartisan support among the American people; we have a Presidency which is responsive. This is uncharacteristic of the last 16-20 years; of a Presidency responding to the immediate interests and demands of the American people. So we better take advantage of this opportunity.

And the global circumstances, with what Russia and China are doing, make it something unprecedented in human history. So really, we've got to think about how we act at this highest level, and immediately, politically in the coming week and weeks ahead.

What Is My Life?

Question: Hello, this is E_____ from Chicago. Well, it's very interesting that this subject, Alexander Hamilton—the way I'm looking at this, personally, is that there were some dramatic changes that happened to me in my life over the last period, and with the fact that I'm going through some health issues, it forced me to really look at the question of what is my life? You know, as an individual, from the standpoint of me being involved with Mr. LaRouche and this organization over the years, that has assisted me greatly, especially in the times that we're in, because I'm really conscious of me being personally responsible.

And I'd just like to share an experience that I had, actually yesterday. I had to go to the VA because I was having some chest problems. I knew that I would probably be there for a while, so I took *The Vision of Alexander Hamilton*. And the doctors and the nurses were commenting on it. So what I did, I had the leaflet where we were getting petitions for President Trump to support Glass-Steagall, and I just said, "OK, well, go to the website," and thus everybody was amenable to that. And that's the way I'm looking at self-activating, because I'm not in a position where I can get out and get to meetings and various things like that, so that's what I've come up with...

The idea is, we have to do whatever we can within whatever our circumstances are, and I'm trying best as I can to further this process. So that's my report.

Steger: That's great. This question you raised on immortality, I think it's a useful exercise, or what Einstein would call a "thought experiment," that everyone should put themselves in the shoes of President Trump, and think about that; by this time you're clearly aware that there are very, very powerful forces that would like to destroy you and your Presidency—and even kill you.

Around John Kennedy, there were a lot of people who were just no damned good—Robert McNamara, McGeorge Bundy, a lot of the people. But Kennedy recognized that there was a different quality, and the President has to have this; Reagan had this. This was what made Reagan special, even though he was dealing with Bush Sr. and James Baker and this whole Bush crowd and the whole Wall Street crowd around Bush. But you've got to come to terms with something about what your life truly means.

Someone like Trump, a President under these circumstances, to fulfill the question of Glass-Steagall, to fulfill this program, he has to go to the most profound characteristics of human identity possible; he has to touch that, the way Beethoven touched it, the way Lincoln grasped that sense of identity. Because that's where you find the strength to overcome this opposition, and to transcend it to a higher level of existence; but the only way a President is capable of doing that, is because there is an engagement with the population that has the same sense of commitment and value of human identity.

And so, I think, it's useful—you have to put your-

self in the position of where do we have to go to accomplish this? And we have to be able to challenge people around us and in the organizing, around these kinds of conceptions, of what does one's life truly mean? I'm sure Dennis can tell the story: one of Lyn's favorite cartoons, was the guy being marched in the casket in the funeral procession, and all of a sudden, he pops up in the casket, and it shows a little bubble, and he says, "What was *that* all about?"

You know, people don't think about what their life really is going to mean, especially at a moment of history like this, where big decisions are going to be made about the long-term characteristic of human existence, on this planet and beyond. And we are now today engaged in a discussion about what's absolutely critical to shape the coming next 500 years. The same way that people shaping the Italian Renaissance, like Nicholas of Cusa and others, were conscious of acting upon a fundamental shift in the nature of human identity and human development; and that we should recognize that this is precious, it's an honor to participate in, and it's a lot of responsibility to fulfill this kind of transformation.

And I think if people go back and read the *Four Laws*, as John Sigerson has suggested, you'll find that this Question is really the subject of discussion, of the *Four Laws*: once you get past the initial introduction, this is the actual content that Mr. LaRouche has always grappled with, and is really the great potency of why a small grouping of people can overcome what seems to be an all-potent political force—and yet, we can bring down Wall Street, we can bring down the British system. And we can transform it into an entirely new system.

So I appreciate your comments, because they're very provocative, and useful contribution.

Question: Hi, this is R____ in Oregon. Mike, could you could review the Trump speech briefly and pick out three or four, or five of the things you found to be most interesting, the high points?

Steger: One of the most important things Trump did, at the beginning of the speech, and it was thoroughly composed from this standpoint, is he came back to the Centennial Fair; he started off with the 250th anniversary of the birth of our nation, in the signing of the Declaration of Independence; and immediately, people were cast out of the immediate crisis, the immediate circumstances that they all think are governing their re-election, or how good they think they look in their white dresses...

So automatically, you're shifted out of the immediate circumstances and you're situated now into something of what is going to be the effect, of what we do here today? And he comes back and recognizes that the effect of Lincoln—because the Exposition in 1876 was clearly the effect of Lincoln's administration—yet, Lincoln was gone, he'd already been killed over a decade earlier.

Breaking Out of Cynicism

But Trump has taken off the lid, in terms our ability. This is something: we have to break out of the cynicism. What Trump's speech did was offer a potential for us to shape the policy; he's enabled us to bring the LaRouche program and the LaRouche policy to bear in the United States. He can't wave a magic wand and make it so, but he can certainly enable us, and that led into that Centennial Fair, these questions of the space program. I mean, you can split hairs on if there's too much discussion of privatization of space or not. We are now discussing in this country, can we get a man or woman back to the Moon; can we get men and women to the Moon by 2019, or will it be 2021?

Now, maybe it was just me, but for the last 8 years, if not 16 years—that was not even possible! And I know NASA's been working on these projects, but certainly for the last eight years under Obama, there was a complete shutdown of *any* of these discussions! And the Curiosity landing on Mars was countervailing against the Obama program, and it was a great success.

An 18-year-old's Perspective

Question: My name is J. and I was at the Congressional meetings yesterday. This is my report, from my perspective, as an 18-year-old. It was my first time lobbying, and when we first got there, we went into the House of Representatives. It was very busy—that was interesting, that post-Trump's speech, that suddenly, everything is buzzing, that the government is actually doing something for once. And then, we

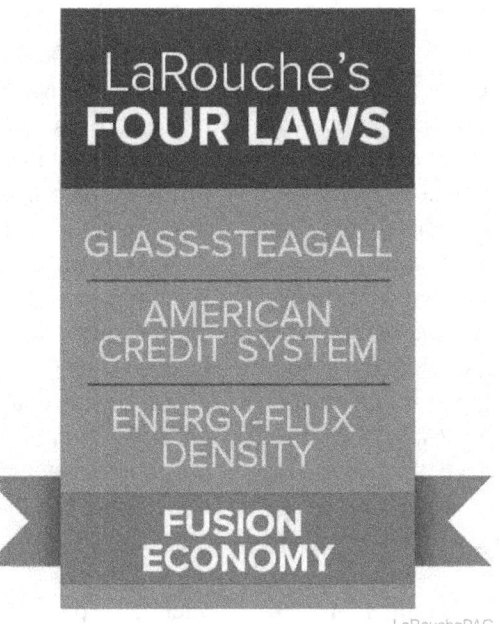

LaRouche's
FOUR LAWS

GLASS-STEAGALL

AMERICAN
CREDIT SYSTEM

ENERGY-FLUX
DENSITY

**FUSION
ECONOMY**

LaRouchePAC

started going around to different Congressmen's offices and talking about Glass-Steagall and the Silk Road.

Some staffers, especially at one meeting, were sort of just listening and taking notes. After about maybe 15 minutes, you can tell, he just tuned out, or "he overloaded." But when you contrast that with our other meeting, with a high-level staffer, he was actually listening very intently. He also knew something about the JFK concert we had done in Boston four years ago, because he is from that state.

He asked towards the end of it, "So, what exactly do you want me to tell the others? What's the most important thing?" And I think it was T. who said, "One, definitely, talk about Glass-Steagall, and talk about these issues," because we were bringing up more than just Glass-Steagall; we were bringing up the Silk Road, because these issues aren't separate, and you can't pass a lot of the infrastructure that Trump proposes without passing Glass-Steagall.

I also was taken aback by how easy it is to just go into these congressmen's offices and just start talking to either them or their staffers. And you can also set up a meeting with them, the day of, or the next day, and we would just give them this information. I really don't understand why people just protest when they can go inside and tell them this.

Steger: That was really refreshing, J. It's true: Our government is so accessible: The ability exists for Americans to shape our destiny and act, especially at this kind of moment, when we've broken free of this fascist system of the last 16 years. There's no other country that I know of where you can engage the government in the way we can. And then, to take it to the level of ideas, I just think that your report was refreshing, and I hope that you stay engaged in the process.

Question: I hope so, especially realizing how easy that was. And knowing that I, or anybody, can walk into their local representative's office: It means that change can be done in this country much easier than people think.

Trump Reflecting on FDR

Steger: You know, it was interesting; there was an interview with President Trump recently, when he was walking around the White House—and you could hear the change in the tone of his voice when he referenced —he said, "You see those ramps right there? That was for Franklin Roosevelt." And you're somewhat struck by the fact that Franklin Roosevelt who pulled us out of the Depression with massive political opposition from within his own party *and* the opposition from Wall Street, and he pulled us out of the Depression, launched major development projects like the TVA and the Grand Coulee and the Hoover Dam, and all the other—the electrification programs, massive jobs works to get people working again? Then he fought two wars against two nations—and he did it all from a wheelchair. And that's—I think when Trump sees those ramps—he recognizes that what you have to be willing to do to fulfill the legacy of this country, requires that kind of devotion, to something much greater in mankind than most people recognize.

So I think we're looking to capture the efforts of Lincoln and Roosevelt, because these people were clearly of a sublime quality in their leadership. That's really what we have to ask of our population, and the platform that we have to provide to this Presidency.

Organizing Everyone

Question: Hi, it's Patrick from Connecticut. I'm just going to follow through with what I've been doing. I've been passing the literature around, and getting the signatures. And I've been talking to a lot of students over the last year, because there's so many kids that are like lost; they have no place to turn except whatever they were told. Anyway, I give 'em the *Four Laws* so they can look at what it means, and how it's going to change the future for them. So whenever I go back to the stores, I ask 'em, "what do you think?" And a lot of them are really, they're happy because they see a future. Otherwise, there's nothing on the other side.

Also I've been crashing Democratic town meetings, passing out the LaRouche's *Four Laws*, and trying to get more people out of that vise-grip they're in. And it's very difficult, but it's not impossible. And whatever I can do; I join groups or organizations so I can work with a lot of people. It's expensive, but in the long run you meet a lot of people.

But I'm continuing to spread the New Paradigm of development and infrastructure. And with that, I end.

Steger: That's excellent. And the participation in this kind of political process is—it's unique. What Mr. LaRouche has created, to have access to this discussion of ideas and political action is a remarkable change in the dimensions of human culture and human society. And we're at the point where action according to these principles and the LaRouche method is of the greatest urgency and the greatest potential effect. Probably the fastest way we can shut down these anti-Trump protesters is to pass Glass-Steagall. This administration, this culture in Congress, we have to educate them now, over the coming weeks, not simply that Glass-Steagall needs to be done, but that they've got to wage a war against the enemies of our country.

We've got to mobilize them toward the higher agenda of putting Glass-Steagall through and launching the kind of development of the country that's possible. There's so much changing. There's an article today in the *San Francisco Chronicle* that says, "California Republicans, the New Party of the Poor?" And basically, the Republican Party out here is realizing hat the only way they're ever going to come back to power is by going to organize the people in the Central Valley, and attacking the massive inequality, the hyperinflation in real estate. You're seeing massive political changes in this country.

And these are the obvious predicates that are changing. The potential is to change the actual sense of human identity. That is what Mr. LaRouche identified back in the 1950s to be the basis for his own unique discovery in economics. It was a similar type of discovery that was made to launch the Florentine Renaissance. We are at that kind of break point, and I think if we take a devotion over this coming week, with as intense an outreach as we can—we've got these pro-Trump rallies on Saturdays throughout the country—I know Diane is going to be participating in one in New Jersey. We can organize people there, and we organize them to create a new American Renaissance, to fulfill what our Founding Fathers had fought and created a new country for, which was to unleash that industrial capability, but also the creative capability of the human mind, in the context of true political freedom.

That's how we're going to end this Obama tyranny, this Bush legacy. We're going to launch a real economic recovery in the United States *and* in the world.

Iran on the Cusp of Multiple Eurasian Land- and Sea-Bridges

by Ramtanu Maitra

March 5—Situated at the southwestern corner of the Eurasian landmass, Iran is perhaps the most well-connected to this landmass and areas beyond. Though blocked off in its east and northeast because of topography and instabilities in Afghanistan and the bordering areas of Pakistan, Iran's uniqueness is a result of its location and history. On its north, it abuts the Caspian Sea while southern Iran is on the Persian Gulf and the Gulf of Oman. To its west, Iran is not only connected by land through Iraq into Arabia, but also because of its borders with Turkey, has a direct link with Europe. Additionally, on its north, Iran has land connections with the South Caucasus flanking the western shores of the Caspian, while it also has a direct land hook-up with Central Asia along the eastern shores of the Caspian. It is this unique location that has helped Iran emerge, in the past, not only as a very important center of civilization, absorbing the cultural fruits that various land and sea-linked countries had to offer, but also as a key trading nation.

In addition to its location and its focus on utilizing the land and sea connectivity with the region and areas beyond, Iran possesses many other ingredients to become a major economic center. Iran has vast reserves of gas and oil, which ensure not only a significant source of export earnings, but also provide stability to its power generation sector, at least in the short and mid-terms. Most

importantly, perhaps, is its cultural and civilizational strength that has helped to develop a core of manpower that can innovate and improve upon technologies required for nation-building.

However, in order to make its people fully productive, Iran has to deal with its increasingly dwindling water sources. It is the threat of a shortfall of water which could lead to serious delays, if not abandonment of many development projects, and which could prevent a more even redistribution of its population. There are reports that the Iran government is aware of the water problem and is planning to deal with it.

Speaking on the sidelines of the groundbreaking ceremony of the Siraf water desalination unit in Bushehr Province last December, Energy Minister Hamid Chitchian had said "plans are in place to provide re-

CC/Arad Mojtahedi

Naghsh-i Jahan Square, the "image of the world," in Isfahan (Esfahan), built in the early 17th Century during the efflorescence of culture under the Safavid dynasty.

gions straddling the southern coasts of Iran, with potable water by building 50 water desalination units," the Islamic Republic News Agency (IRNA) reported. Those plants will be built in different areas adjacent to the Persian Gulf and Sea of Oman. Also, in April 2015, the deputy head of the Atomic Energy Organization of Iran (AEOI), Behrouz Kamalvandi, had told the Iranian media that Tehran is planning to build small nuclear power plants and desalination facilities in the southern part of the country.

What Made Iran a Special Place

Ancient Iran, known as Persia, had taken full advantage of these land and cultural linkages, particularly the land links. The Achaemenian Empire in Persia in the 6th and 5th Century B.C., stretched as far as Libya to the West, and extended beyond what is now the Afghanistan-Pakistan border in the east. In its northeast, it bordered the Aral Sea while in its northwest, it covered most of Greece. The expansion of the Persian Empire had its downsides as well. It provoked and attracted invaders.

The geographical identity that defines Iran today, was subjected to a myriad of invasions beginning in 330 B.C. by

1. Alexander of Macedon;
2. Skirmishes with the Scythians of the southern Caucasus, to its northwest;
3. The Arab invasion in the 7th Century, leading to the Islamization of Iran;
4. The Turkic Seljuk tribe from its west in the 11th Century, and;
5. Mongols, who believed in Shamanism or Buddhism and opposed Islamic tenets, in the 13th Century.

However, some of these 'invasions' did not always lead to the conquest of Persia/Iran, but more often integrated people from the bordering nations, leading to the enrichment and embellishment of Persia's/Iran's culture and overall improvement of the Persian people.

The explosion in literature, architecture, art and poetry during the 17th and 18th Century Persia/Iran under the Safavids, seen particularly in Isfahan, a capital of the empire for a period, was perhaps the legacy of Iran's historical past.

"The Safavids were Turkicized Iranians, probably of Kurdish origin, whose power base was among the Turkic tribesmen in northwestern Iran, Anatolia (Turkey) and parts of Syria. Safavids built their capital at Tabriz in Iran. Timurlane's culture has held sway at Isfahan since then."

The History of Iran cannot be defined in the context of the landmass that defines Iran's territory today. But it does define the cultural and civilizational backbone of the Iranian people as a whole. For instance, many western historians identify Ibn Sina, al Biruni, Khwarazmi, al-Farabi, al-Ghazali and many others who have shined their intellectual light over a vast area in the past, as Arabs. In reality, they were all products, and benefactors of what the Persian/Iranian civilization had to offer. While the Arab origins of some of them are on record, the influence upon them of the civilizational splendors spread by all those who settled in Persia cannot be denied.

Silk Road Then…and Once More The Trading Hub

With this wide access to the Eurasian landmass in the pre- and post-Christian era, the Persian/Iranian nation had, unlike any other nation at the time, also led

Tasnim

The first cargo train from China arrived in Tehran in February 2016, after covering a distance of almost 10,000 kilometers.

to the development of various trade routes and what was then called the Silk Road. "In Iran, the Silk Road was of special importance. Considering the role of silk in ancient times, it can be said that the history of Iran and the Silk Road were intertwined. The Silk Road connected old centers of Iranian civilization that were located along the route. The trade and cultural exchange between the two great countries of Iran and China were carried out via the Silk Road... By playing a key role in the Silk Road, Iran made great contributions to the booming of the silk trade and to the exportation of this commodity to the West. During the Parthian era, the Silk Road was still an important route for the exchange of commodities between various countries." [See previous link].

During the Parthian era, which the historians identify as between 247 BC to 224 AD, "Iran had signed the first trade agreement with China, which was under the rule of the Huns. Chang Ki Yen was the head of a 100-man delegation that visited Iran. In his account of his travel to Iran, he gave some very interesting information about life in the Parthian Empire. He wrote about a region located on the shores of the 'Western Sea' [Caspian Sea]. He said that the people of the region dedicated their time to farming. They were especially good at cultivating rice." [See previous link].

Jumping almost 2000-plus years forward, it was noted that Iran finalized a cooperation agreement with China last November which would allow Chinese traders to use Iranian territory for exports to Europe. The agreement, which was signed between customs offi-

cials of Iran and China, is part of an ambitious Chinese plan to revive the ancient Silk Road and bring it one step closer to reality, added the *Iran Daily News* report, citing IRNA.

This old Silk Road connection between China and Iran was revived physically in February last year when a train, carrying 32 containers of commercial products from eastern Zhejiang province, took 14 days to make the 9,500-kilometre journey zig-zagging through Kazakstan and Turkmenistan. "The arrival of this train in less than 14 days is unprecedented," said the head of the Iranian railway company, Mohsen Pourseyed Aqayi. The revival of the Silk Road is crucial for the countries on its route," he said at a ceremony at Tehran's rail station attended by the ambassadors of China and Turkmenistan. The journey was 30 days shorter than the sea voyage from Shanghai to the Iranian port of Bandar Abbas, according to Aqayi.

The arrival of the train from Zhejiang was widely welcomed in Iran, but the route it followed also exhibited the limitation of the old Silk Road, or the variations of it that exist today. Such limitations exist for a number of reasons, some of which are entirely geopolitical, while some others are a result of the security mess that exists today in the Eurasian landmass, thanks to centuries of conflicts and confrontations brewed by the contesting colonial empires, particularly British Empire.

North-South Integration of the Eurasian Land-Mass

One such shortcoming, as of now, is that the Eurasian landmass is inter-linked by a ribbon-like transport corridor that runs north of the landmass and then dips somewhat tentatively (again, restricted by geopolitical wrestling of the powers-that-be that evokes conflicts and dissensions within the participating nations) from east to west, linking China to the Caspian Sea. The transport corridor dips southward heading into Iran. But the Eurasian landmass is almost 3,500 km in length, calculating from the China-Russia borders to Pakistan's coast. What the British geopolitician Halford Mackinder, working to promote an unfettered expansion of the British Empire, sometimes through brutal con-

A railway viaduct on the Rasht-Astara section of the INSTC nears completion.

Iran Daily

The Qazvin-Rasht-Astara segment of the railroad, to be finished this year, will complete the INSTC land route.

to notice that there is a consecutive vertical row of countries of Eurasia from Russia in the north to India in the south (Central Asian countries, Iran, Pakistan) that does not yet link either with the east or with the west. I would call this continuous belt of countries situated along the meridian of the center of Eurasia the 'belt of anticipation.'

Sengupta pointed out in her treatise, Logistical Spaces IV: Connectivity as the New Asian Paradigm [see link above]:

Nazarbayev's 'belt of anticipation' is interesting, particularly since it indicates a vertical definition of the Eurasian space that is generally visualized as a horizontal expanse. This is essentially the logistical vision of a landlocked state which wishes to move out of the confines of traditional east-west routes of transportation. Much of the transportation linking Asia to Europe was historically conceptualized as east-west epitomized by the Silk Route. Of course this east-west corridor frequently had smaller north-south off shoots leading to southern ports.

Despite those obvious shortcomings, Iran, in addition to developing a rail-link to China through Turkmenistan and Uzbekistan to its north, is on the verge of making the north-south land transport corridor through Central Asia (eastern shores of the Caspian Sea), South Caucasus (along the western shores of the Caspian) and over the Caspian's water using fully functional ships and barges. Moreover, Iran's southeastern port of Chabahar on the Gulf of Oman is now getting fully developed to link up with India's west coast by sea and has attracted Afghanistan to become a part of this land-sea corridor.

Development of the International North-South Transport Corridor (INSTC), a multi-modal transportation route, was officially agreed upon in the year 2000 by Iran, Russia, and India at a meeting in St. Petersburg.

quests, and then its preservation in the 20th Century, identified this area as the crucial hinterland that the Empire must brace itself to control. The Eurasian landmass actually extends from northern Xinjiang province of China, across the deserts and pastures through the mountain ranges along China's western borders with Kazakstan, to the Arabian Sea, Gulf of Oman and Persian Gulf in the south. This is the heart of the Eurasian landmass. Once reintegrated, it will bring back those glorious yesteryears of Iran.

This was reflected in Kazak President Nursultan Nazarbayev's definition of Eurasia. He argued back in the 1990s:

If we look at a geographical map then it is easy

In essence, this corridor is designed to link South Asia, and the west coast ports of some Southeast Asian nations to Europe and Central Asia via the Indian Ocean and Persian Gulf to the Caspian Sea running through Iran, Azerbaijan, and then through the Russian Federation to northern Europe.

The route is not fully ready yet. However, as per the recommendations of the 5th Coordination Council meeting of INSTC held in Baku, Azerbaijan, in 2013, a dry-run of the INSTC was successfully conducted by the Federation of Freight Forwarders of India (FFFAI) in 2014 on the routes; 1) from Nhava Sheva (Mumbai), to Bandar Abbas (Iran), to Tehran-Bandar Anzali (Iran) to Astrakan (Russia); and 2) from Nhava Sheva (Mumbai), to Bandar Abbas (Iran), to Baku (Azerbaijan).

As of now, the Asian trade travelling by INSTC unloads at Bandar Abbas, situated on the Persian Gulf, and then travels by rail to Qazvin (Iran) and then by road to Bandar Anzali to get loaded on a ship crossing the Caspian Sea (south to north) to get unloaded at Astrakan in the Russian Federation. From Astrakan, the cargo becomes rail freight travelling to northern Europe. That is where it stands now. But within a few years that could change.

Now that Iran has been unshackled from sanctions, the INSTC is going to be ready in 2019. The difficult part in the INSTC land route is unloading and reloading a number of times between Qazvin, Bandar Anzali, and Astrakan. This wastes time and money. However, this bottleneck will be removed later this year when Iran completes the building of this stretch. The railroad from Qazvin to Rasht runs through a mountain pass to bring the trade route to the southwestern corner of the Cas-

Iran Visitor

Above: Looking down on Bandar Anzali, close to Rasht. It is Iran's Caspian Sea port.

Left: The Port of Astara, where Iran meets Azerbaijan, has been integrated into the INSTC.

CC/Samaksasanian

pian Sea, and then will extend along the western shore of the Caspian to Astara, bordering Azerbaijan. On the Azerbaijan side of the border, the linking town has the same name, Astara. These two towns are getting linked-up by a small stretch of railroad. The construction of the Rasht to Astara stretch of railroad on the Iranian side has begun.

The good news is that the railroad has been given the proverbial green light by the head of the Iranian railways, Mohsen Pour Seyed Aghaie. On Jan 12, 2016, *Trend News Agency* reported that Aghaie said that "the construction of the Rasht-Astara railway will begin in 2016 and finish in 2019." The Qazvin-Rasht part of the railroad will be completed in 2017. In 2015, the railway companies of Iran, Azerbaijan, and Russia had signed a document to expedite construction of this 75 km-long Qazvin-Rasht-Astara railroad project.

In addition, the INSTC plans to develop some important spurs. One of them, already in place, is the

Iran's Chabahar Port on the Gulf of Oman.

The Iran Project

Iranian President Dr. Hassan Rouhani, welcoming the agreement, said on that occasion that connectivity is at the heart of this agreement. The development of Chabahar Port, and the free trade zone along with the 500-km rail-linkage between Chabahar and Zahedan, an Iranian city close to the Iran-Pakistan border, has the potential to benefit all three countries immensely. India has already built the 220-km Zaranj-Delaram highway—also known as Route 606—in 2009 which provides a direct road access to Afghanistan's Garland Highway. A highway link between Zahedan and Zaranj, a town in Afghanistan's Nimruz province, also exists.

930-km rail link, running from Uzen in the oil and gas-rich western Kazakstan through Turkmenistan to the existing railroad in Gorgan in northwestern Iran, running close to the southeastern coast of the Caspian Sea. This link, begun in Dec 2014, enables Iran and Turkmenistan to link with China and the Pacific Ocean through Kazakstan.

An apparent constraint of the INSTC at this point is the limitations of Iran's Bandar Abbas port to handle a significant growth in cargo-handling. Full-fledged utilization of INSTC will not be possible unless the expansion of the port is undertaken. Another weakness of the INSTC is its lack of linkages with Afghanistan.

Chabahar Port to Link-up with Asia East of Iran

While the INSTC is a north-south linkage between southernmost part of Iran to the South Caucasus and Central Asia by railroad, the other major economic development project to build connections in Iran is the development of Chabahar port, including building a free-trade industrial zone around the port. On May 23, 2016, the heads of state of Iran, Afghanistan, and India signed a trilateral agreement at Tehran to develop Chabahar Port located on the Gulf of Oman in the southeastern Iranian province of Sistan-Balochistan.

The development of Chabahar Port will cut transportation costs and time between Iran and India's ports on its western coast by almost a third. Moreover, the access to Chabahar Port, and to Zahedan further north,

Tehran Times

Iran's key oil and gas facilities are concentrated in the western half of the country.

The Dasht-e-Lut is one of the driest and hottest places on Earth.

will enable India to reach four major Afghan cities, Kabul, Kandahar, Heart, and Mazar-e-Sharif, through Afghanistan's Garland Highway.

India's state-run Oil and Natural Gas Corporation (ONGC) stated in April, 2016 that it was open to a $20 billion investment in petrochemicals and fertilizer plants, an LNG plant, and a natural gas cracker in the Chabahar free trade zone. These investments would facilitate the flow of Iranian and potentially Central Asian natural gas to support India's growing energy demand. The same logic likely applies for Japanese and other energy security-minded investors. For their part, the Japanese have already expressed interest in investing in the port."

A Physical Constraint To Overcome

Located in one of the most arid zones of this world, Iran is divided into six key and 31 secondary catchment areas. "Besides the Persian Gulf and Gulf of Oman Basins, all of Iran's basins are located in the interior, where renewable freshwater sources are limited. Close to half of Iran's total renewable water is located in the Persian Gulf and Gulf of Oman Basins, representing one quarter of its land mass. Conversely, the Markazi Basin covers more than half of Iran's land mass, but holds less than one-third of the available freshwater."

What makes the alleviation of Iran's water-shortage particularly challenging is the fact that "Iran is mountainous; more than half of the country is at altitudes between 1,000—2,000 meters and 16% of the territory is above 2,000 meters with some mountains of 3,000-4,000 meters."

Damavand Mount at 5,670 meters is the highest in west Asia and Europe. Some 11,000 square kilometers—equal to 0.9% of the land at the Caspian Sea coast—is below sea level. In the Central Plateau the lowest point in the Dasht-e-Lut [one of the hottest places on earth where surface temperature registers 160 degree Fahrenheit—Ed] is 156 meters. The mean altitude of the country is approximately 1,250 meters and that of the Central Plateau 900 meters.

In the Sefid-Rud valley [Sefid-Rud is a river that makes a water gap through the Alborz mountain range. It then widens the valley between the Talesh Hills and the main Alborz range, enabling a major route between Tehran and Gīlān Province with its Caspian lowlands. In the wide valley before the Sefid-Rud enters the Caspian Sea south of Rasht a number of transportation and irrigation canals have been cut—Ed] as a result of the low altitude, dry winds from the interior move towards Guilan, creating an area of low rainfall which extends up to some 40 kilometers from Rasht (capital of Guilan Province). The great chain of Alborz and Zagros forms a "V shaped" natural barrier which inhibits the humid winds of the southwest and prevents the majority of clouds from reaching the center of the country, so steppes and deserts are created.

II. Obama the British Traitor

Good at Killing

by Carl Osgood

March 4—Barack Obama was trained and indoctrinated in killing by his stepfather Lolo Soetoro, who was a colonel in the Indonesian army during the 1965-66 Indonesian massacres which a top-secret CIA report called "one of the worst mass murders of the 20th century." Wikipedia, citing various academic books and newspaper articles, reports:

> The killings were done "face to face," unlike the mechanical methods of killing used by Nazi Germany. The methods of killing included shooting, dismembering alive and beheading with Japanese-style samurai swords. Islamic extremists often paraded severed heads on spikes. Corpses were often thrown into rivers, and at one point officials complained to the Army that the rivers running into the city of Surabaya were clogged with bodies. In areas such as Kediri in East Java, Nahdlatul Ulama youth wing (Ansor) members lined up Communists, cut their throats and disposed of the bodies in rivers. Rows of severed penises were often left behind as a reminder to the rest. The killings left whole sections of villages empty, and

the houses of victims or the interned were looted and often handed over to the military.

Obama's own autobiography, *Dreams from My Father,* reports some of what his stepfather taught him about murder soon after these events.[1]

Barack Obama is a killer. He was a killer from the moment he first stepped into the Oval Office in January 2009, remained a killer throughout his entire eight years in office, is a killer today, and will remain a killer as long as he lives. Presidents throughout U.S. history have made decisions that resulted in death, particularly decisions to dispatch U.S. armed forces, and Obama did that more than once throughout his time in office. But unlike any previous President, Obama personally chose people for assassination again and again—men and women picked from a list presented to him every Tuesday by his national security apparatus.

Obama personally decided who on those lists would live, and who would die. Obama's weapon of choice was the armed drone, either the Predator or its larger

---

1. See *EIR,* Feb. 19, 2016, p. 35.

U.S. Air Force

Above: U.S. Reaper drone shooting a missile.

Left: Ex-President Obama in the situation room.

Pete Souza/White House

cousin the Reaper, firing Hellfire missiles at whoever fell into the cross hairs of its operators half a world away. Obama is personally responsible for the death of every single person killed in this manner, regardless of whether he or she were on his secret death list, or just happened to be in the wrong place at the wrong time. Americans must face the fact that, for eight years, we tolerated a crazed murderer in our highest office.

The fact of Obama's Tuesday kill sessions was first revealed by the *New York Times* on May 29, 2012. Obama, the *Times* reported, had placed himself at the helm of a top secret "nominations" process to designate terrorists for kill or capture—though in reality, "kill" had become the preferred action. The *Times* characterized Obama as "the liberal law professor who campaigned against the Iraq war and torture," but who now "insisted on approving every new name on an expanding 'kill list,' poring over terrorist suspects' biographies on what one official called the macabre 'baseball cards' of an unconventional war."

It was through this process that American citizen Anwar al-Awlaki came into Obama's sights. The decision to kill him—without trial—Obama told colleagues, was an "easy one." Retired Adm. Dennis Blair, who was Director of National Intelligence until May 2010, told the *Times* that the intense focus on drone strikes drowned out any discussion of an actual, long term strategy against Al-Qaeda. "The steady refrain in the White House was, 'This is the only game in town'—[it] reminded

Muhammad ud-Deen
Imam Anwar al-Awlaki in Yemen, October 2008.

The Intercept *website.*

me of body counts in Vietnam," said Blair, who began his military service during that war.

Anyone Nearby Is Killed

But it wasn't only those people whose names Obama picked out of the list that were killed. Sometimes the chosen victims were caught on lonely desert roads in between villages, but not always. Innocent civilians were often caught by the explosions, though the numbers are uncertain because, in part, the Obama Administration adopted ways of obscuring the actual death toll. One way was to deem all military age males who were killed because they happened to be in the vicinity, as "enemy killed in action," or EKIA for short, unless explicit intelligence arose afterwards exonerating them.

A videotape was made of every drone killing, and it has been reported that Obama watched and rewatched them in the closed-off private room in the White House where he also spent long hours watching sports events—as the strangling of the July 1944 plotters was filmed for the *Führer*. The victims of Obama's killings were always referred to as "bug-splat."

About three and a half years after the *New York Times* account, more details emerged on the Tuesday kill-sessions when an anonymous insider divulged classified documents to *The Intercept* that were then published in a series of reports led by investigative reporter Jeremy Scahill. The source told Scahill that he believed that the public had a right to understand how the kill-lists function, and how people were ultimately assassinated by Presidential order. "This outrageous explosion of watch-listing—of monitoring people and racking and stacking them on lists, assigning them numbers, assigning them 'baseball cards,' assigning them death sentences without notice, on a worldwide battlefield—was, from the very first instance, wrong," the source said.

The documents that *The Intercept* published, not only confirmed what had earlier been reported in the *New York Times* but provided additional details as to how the kill machine, which Obama was overseeing, was being built and institutionalized. "Taken together, the secret documents lead to the conclusion that Washington's 14-year high-value targeting campaign suffers from an over-reliance on signals intelligence, an apparently incalculable civilian toll, and—due to a preference for assassination rather than capture—an inability to extract potentially valuable intelligence from terror suspects," Scahill wrote. In fact, what was happening was that assassination was being normalized as a "tool" of counterterrorism.

One of the features exposed in the documents was the extent of the process itself and the chain of command, by which names proposed to be reviewed by the President, made their way up through to the Tuesday meetings. For Somalia and Yemen, the process started at a military unit within the Joint Special Operations Command called TF 48-4, where military operators and specialists from other agencies would build the case for targeting a specific person for death. From there, the intelligence "package" on that person would be passed on to either U.S. Africa Command, for Somalia, or U.S. Central Command for Yemen, then on to the Joint Chiefs of Staff and the Secretary of Defense. After that, it would be examined by the Principals Committee of the National Security Council and their deputies.

The Intercept noted that while there were various accounts of how this bureaucratic process functioned, they all stressed the role of John O. Brennan, who had

Pete Souza/White House

President Obama being briefed by his chief counterterrorism adviser John Brennan. Brennan later became director of the CIA.

been Obama's counterterrorism advisor in the White House, before Obama appointed him CIA director in 2013. Brennan concentrated control over the nominations process in the White House.

Regardless of the role of Brennan, in every single instance, it was Obama who made the decision to put someone's name on the kill list and who signed off on it. In other words, every single person killed by Obama's drone program, was authorized for assassination by the President himself.

The process was of course a total violation of the Constitution. Aside from the fact that the United States was committing acts of war, in countries that it was not at war with, in violation of the Constitutional requirement for Congressional authorization, there was also the matter of the targeted killings of American citizens. The case of Anwar al-Awlaki is illustrative. Awlaki was killed ostensibly because of his relationship to Al-Qaeda, but he was killed without a trial, which every American is entitled to. However, he might have been an FBI informant carrying certain secrets about the targeting program—and might have even known about U.S. government ties to Al-Qaeda—but that story has yet to be fully told.

More Americans Murdered

But Awlaki wasn't the only American known to have been killed by Obama. Samir Khan, another American, was killed along with Awlaki when a Hellfire missile hit their vehicle in October 2011. Khan was not an "intended target," however. Two weeks later, Awlaki's son, 16-year-old Abdulrahman Awlaki, was killed while having dinner with his cousins and some friends. Immediately after the

Seventeen innocent civilians killed by a U.S. drone in Ra'ada, Yemen, in 2013.

strike, reported *The Intercept*, anonymous U.S. officials asserted that the younger Awlaki was connected to al-Qaeda and was twenty-one years old. When the family produced his birth certificate, the United States changed its position, and an anonymous official called the killing of the teenager an "outrageous mistake."

According to its own publicly released documents, the Obama Administration claimed that a targeted assassination decision had to meet three criteria:

1. Near certainty that the terrorist target is present;
2. Near certainty that non-combatants will not be injured or killed;
3. An assessment that capture is not feasible at the time of the operation.

Yet, it appears that the Administration violated its own criteria repeatedly. One of the slides published by *The Intercept* depicts the results of an operation in Afghanistan, called Haymaker, covering the period from Jan. 1, 2012 to Feb. 28, 2013. The slide reports 219 killed in 56 drone strikes, but only 35 were designated targets. That is, 5 out of every 6 people killed were not "targeted" persons. During one five-month period in that campaign, the ratio was 9 out of 10.

The intelligence source who provided the documents to *The Intercept* said that in remote locations, labeling the dead as "enemies" until proven otherwise was commonplace. The process, he said, often depended on assumptions or best-guesses in remote provinces of Afghanistan or Pakistan—particularly if the dead were "military age males" (MAM). "If there is no evidence that proves a person killed in a strike was either not a MAM, or was a MAM but not an unlawful enemy combatant, then there is no question," he said. They label them "enemies killed in action (EKIA)."

From there, it was only a short step to "signature strikes," where the criteria allowed the targeting of people not based on who they were—which wasn't known—but on patterns of activity. This may explain why weddings were frequent targets. Weddings featured military age males firing guns into the air, a common practice in tribal weddings.

In 2014, former commander of U.S. Central Command Gen. (ret.) John Abizaid, and Georgetown law professor Rosa Brooks, who had served in the Pentagon during the first Obama Administration, issued a report warning that there were tremendous uncertainties in drone warfare and that these uncertainties "are multiplied further when the United States relies on intelligence and other targeting information provided by a host nation government. How can we be sure we are not being drawn into a civil war, or being used to target the domestic political enemies of the host state leadership?"

In other words, the murder program was completely out of control and off the charts, but, as *The Intercept* report shows, it was embraced by Obama very early in his first term, facilitated not only by John Brennan, but also by then-CIA Director Michael Hayden. The fact is, a massive number of crimes were committed. And the official documents, including those classified documents leaked to *The Intercept*, make it clear that there was an absolutely unambiguous chain of command that led straight to Barack Obama.

Pete Souza/White House

Vice President Joe Biden and President Obama (on left), with national security team, Secretary of State Hillary Clinton and Secretary of Defense Robert Gates (seated right front), John Brennan and National Intelligence Director James Clapper (standing extreme right), receiving an update on the operation against Osama bin Laden, the day before bin Laden was killed.

And before he left office, Obama moved to formally institutionalize the killing machine he had honed to a fine edge. On Dec. 5, 2016, the Obama White House released a number of documents which, it claimed, "help to demonstrate that the United States acts consistently with our values and all applicable law, including the law of armed conflict and international human rights law." The first of the newly released documents was a Presidential memorandum that "directs national security departments and agencies to prepare a formal report that describes key legal and policy frameworks currently guiding the United States' use of military force and related national security operations, such as detention, transfer, and interrogation operations." Accompanying the memorandum was a 60-page report which "provides in one place an articulation of the legal and policy frameworks which previously have been found across numerous speeches, public statements, reports, and other materials."

Despite these lies, the truth is that the Obama Administration, over eight years, bombed seven different countries without Constitutionally required Congressional authorization and without any substantive Con-

gressional scrutiny, instead relying, as the 60-page report showed, on the 2001 Authorization to Use Military Force (AUMF), passed by Congress in the immediate aftermath of the 9/11 attacks. Obama said repeatedly over the course of 2016 that he wanted to institutionalize the policies that have governed his Administration's use of force, in hope that this would serve future administrations, and better position the public to judge the actions of government. Obama's intent, in other words, is that the killing machine that he had constructed over the last eight years, go on killing.

But drones aren't the only way, not even the main way that America has become a killing machine since 9/11. "Drone warfare aside, Americans should be appalled by how many people their elected government has directly or indirectly killed since the War on Terror began nearly 15 years ago," wrote former CIA officer Philip Giraldi in a June 2016 article in the *American Conservative*. Giraldi usefully included the second and third order effects of these U.S. wars, effects resulting from the destruction of medical care and infrastructure, which produce enormous casualties, probably many more than die from direct kinetic effects. The total death toll so far could range from 2 to 4 million, Giraldi reports. "The past 15 years have institutionalized and validated the killing process."

III. Lyndon LaRouche in 2000

Politics as Art

by Lyndon H. LaRouche, Jr.
November 6, 2000

Some winced or giggled, when the amiable and gifted Senator Eugene McCarthy conducted political campaigning as poetry-reading sessions. I laugh happily at what he did. Senator McCarthy's critics did not remember, as I do, that President Lincoln had won a terrible, justified, and absolutely necessary war on behalf of all humanity, by aid of lessons adduced from Shakespeare, which he had taught, as directives, to the members of his Cabinet. No one, friend or foe, laughed at the awesome result of that instruction.

Real politics, as Plato and the recently elevated, great, and martyred English statesman Thomas More rightly understood,[1] is properly practiced as a form of Classical art, practiced according to the same principles which the greatest tragedians, Shakespeare and his successor Schiller, most notably, subsequently expressed as Classical modes of composition and performance of poetry and tragedy. To become efficiently literate in history and politics, you must recognize the tragedies composed by those two latter, greatest masters of that art, as no mere fiction, but, like the greatest operatic staging of the tragedies from Shakespeare[2] and Schiller, by Giuseppe Verdi, or, earlier, the relevant operas of Wolfgang Mozart, and Beethoven's **Fidelio**,[3] the authentic, and inspiring representation of the essence of the specific crises in real history to which those compositions refer.

Tomorrow, U.S. election-day, November 7, 2000, we shall witness an awful real-life tragedy on the world stage, the threat, if not yet the actuality of a new dark age. That threat is today's outgrowth of a long-standing, widespread violation of those Classical principles of statecraft which every citizen should have been given the right to know, something that citizen should have known by no later than the time he or she had completed a secondary education.

My life's professional work, during more than fifty years to date, has been focussed on precisely that subject-matter so urgently needed under today's conditions of global crisis: the interdependency of the history of politics and economics with those Classical methods which underlie competence in both art and science.

Lately, I had been prompted by a number of developments, especially because of the increasingly acute quality of the onrushing world crisis, to place much heavier emphasis on my students' and co-workers' rigorous mastery of that function of Classical art. Here, I consolidate and recapitulate what I have said in the content of unpublished manuscripts which were recently written for those collaborators' private use. I do this here, in as popular a form as competent exposition per-

---

1. "Apostolic Letter of Pope John Paul II, Proclaiming St. Thomas More as Patron of Statesmen and Politicians." This was issued, and presented by the Pope, to the Nov. 4-5, 2000 "Jubilee" Conference of Parliamentarians, which drew 5,000 elected officials from 96 nations to Rome.

2. Shakespeare's Richard III is premised on the in-depth account of that turning-point in English history, supplied by Thomas More's guardian's first-hand and related accounts of the actual history of those events. It was through the work of Sir Thomas More himself that Shakespeare acquired the relevant knowledge of that part of English history.

3. Based on the true-life account of the imprisonment and freeing of that Marquis de Lafayette who had been endungeoned at Olmütz on the orders of British Prime Minister Pitt (Beethoven's "Pizzaro"), by courtesy of the Austro-Hungarian Chancellor, and Mozart adversary, von Kaunitz.

Abraham Lincoln and William Shakespeare (inset).
"President Lincoln had won a terrible, justified, and absolutely necessary war on behalf of all humanity, by aid of lessons adduced from Shakespeare, which he had taught, as directives, to the members of his Cabinet."

mits. I do this for the benefit of you as a member of an, unfortunately, still largely unwitting population, a population which the aftermath of this election would tend to overwhelm with despair, unless you are informed of those certain means of remedial action which I outline for you here.

I offer you thus a method for action, which contains the much-needed Classical alternative to today's real-life tragedy of our nation. I present that to you here, with the intent to afford you a guide to the means by which we may escape from the awful consequences, into which the immediate aftermath of a brutish electoral farce, now threatens to plunge our nation, and also the world at large.

For you, if you are a typical adolescent or adult who has good intentions toward mankind in general, I emphasize, that the beginning of the practice of those kinds of real politics which are consistent with your intentions, is to be found in the proper, truthful, but too rarely used form for conducting ordinary discussion. By ordinary discussion, I mean the practical use of that elementary knowledge of the principles of Classical art, which should inform and guide the way in which two acquaintances might converse about anything but trivial housekeeping subjects, on a street-corner, or under almost any other ordinary, or exceptional auspices.

The model you must come to know, to be able to rise to that higher level of deliberation on the subjects of our nation's policy-making issues, is the model to be found in re-enacting the Socratic dialogues of Plato, viewing those dialogues for what they are: Classical dramas portraying exchanges among characters typifying notable actual figures from the living history of the Greece of that age. It is by re-enacting those dialogues as dramas, that ordinary people, may be pleasantly surprised to touch something of that quality of mind which makes for genius, as they become, through experience, increasingly efficient, even as ordinary citizens, in use of the most important principles for rational selection of political choices. From that standpoint, you will also come to know, that every form of important Classical artistic composition, functions according to exactly the same principle as Plato's Socratic method.

Classical composition so defined, includes the greatest works in Classical sculpture and Classical Renaissance painting, such as that of Leonardo da Vinci, Raphael Sanzio, and Rembrandt. It includes all of the greatest Classical poetry and drama. It includes all great musical compositions, which are either Classical from the outset, or rendered fully expressive of Classical principles of composition, by aid of the kind of polish supplied to the Negro Spiritual by the collaboration of

Baritone William Warfield recites a poem at a conference of the Schiller Institute and International Caucus of Labor Committees, Jan. 17, 1998.

Antonin Dvořák and Harry Burleigh, and by the continuation of that process of perfection by the great Classical artist Roland Hayes and his collaborators and followers.

That latter choice of example, the case of the Negro Spiritual, has special importance for all among our people, of African descent or not, who are oppressed by the sense that life has reduced the common folk to the treatment intended for under-dogs, or people degraded even to the social status of virtual human cattle.

If you once come to know the way in which the Classical principle of composition is expressed in such an excellent and profound way by those Spirituals, you should recall that these originated as works of art composed by, and shared among successive generations of cruelly oppressed slaves who were each, at least partially, of African descent. The power of these compositions, which Dvořák, Burleigh, Hayes, and others, have honed to a state of relative perfection, expressed, among those slaves, the same genius inherent in all human beings. Those Spirituals, so honed, have a special power for all, on that account; they should inspire us to recognize, that there is no oppression so efficient, that it can obliterate the fact of the noble quality of humanity, as man and woman made in the image of the Creator, a quality innate to each newborn child.

Typical of the same universal principle, is the celebrated Prisoners' Chorus of Ludwig Beethoven's **Fidelio**, or the chorus of the slaves, *Va Pensiero*, from Giuseppe Verdi's **Nabucco**. The latter chorus became the unofficial national anthem of modern Italy, out of popular recognition of the specific quality of patriotic passion, which that chorus conveys by Classical artistic means. As the case of "Little Boy" illustrates this point best to me, the performances of the repertoire of the Spiritual by Roland Hayes, as by Marion Anderson, set a standard of comparison among those who worked with and followed them, for conveying the Negro Spiritual as a part of the body of mankind's treasure of true Classical art. No respectable musician or Classical actor would disagree.

The underlying principles expressed by the most successful expressions of great Classical artistic composition, are those expressed in the most concentrated form in Plato's dialogues, and in those forms of modern Classical artistic composition which I have broadly identified above.

For reasons which I shall clarify in the pages which follow, the achievements of the Negro Spiritual to such effect, reveal to us today the profound, uniquely human creative power, that power which touches the quality of genius, inhering in each new-born slave of those many generations, who suffered such cruelty at the hands of those who express that same contempt for humanity, which was exhibited by what the followers of Richard M. Nixon launched, in collaboration with the Ku Klux Klan, as that legacy of the old Confederacy called the "Southern Strategy" of 1966-1968. That wicked, inhuman legacy of the Nixon campaign, is the same cultural corruption running rampant in the Congress, in our national electoral processes, and in practiced U.S. foreign policy today. It is the same evil, as revived so today, which the voice of the slave indicts, as if by a voice speaking from across the centuries, through the Classical form of the Negro Spiritual. When we participate in such music, or other Classical art, we are similarly inspired, and strengthened in our commitment to wage the battle for all humanity, as all true followers of Jesus Christ have done.

The successful composition and performance of such Classical artistry, depends upon a certain method, that Socratic method most efficiently illustrated by Plato's dialogues. This is a method for locating, cultivating, and applying that noble authority which is embed-

Percy Bysshe Shelley: "Poets are the unacknowledged legislators of the universe."

ded in human nature from birth, our innate authority sometimes identified as creative reason. It is when we communicate with one another in this way, on matters which the poet Shelley described as "profound and impassioned conceptions respecting man and nature," that that power of reason born within us, may be willfully aroused, and shared with others. So, were our citizens not so often foolish, we would always rely on that method, for assembling with others to shape the policies and future destiny of our nation, and its relations with other nations.

It is that potential power for Classical artistic communication, which you must summon from within yourself, for your deliberations with your fellow-citizens on those policy-issues. That is the method you should choose, which will presently determine the present moments' choice between recovery, and a living nightmare for not only our nation, but for most of the world.

My central objective in writing his report, is to make that point clear to you in particular. If you understand that point, we shall succeed, together, in bringing the class of those who continue to occupy the role of politicians, up to that higher moral level, too.

1. Why Americans Usually Lie

Begin by asking yourself: What should the word "truth" be understood as signifying? To answer that question, begin by peeking into typical scenes of relevant misbehavior, those prevalent among both leading political figures and ordinary citizens, as we have seen these echoed, yet once again, during the now concluding national election-campaign.

As all of us who are adults, and who are honest about what we know, recall, that, with the most extremely rare individual exceptions, virtually every American, including those who claim to be devoutly religious, is an impulsive liar. He, or she will lie, almost instinctively, as the typically depraved members of "debaters' clubs" do, and as certain popular political candidates do, "to win the argument," "to get my way." Of these, those hypocrites who call themselves Christians, are not the worst cases, but, all too frequently, only the most disgusting ones.

In families in which households still exist these perilous days, children continue to witness their parents politely lying to the guests, the guests lying similarly in return, and both parents and guests hailing each other at the close of the visit, "We must do this soon again!" Then, according to popular custom, follows the epilogue, in which the children may overhear their parents' ridicule and even calumnies, directed against the guests they had just, a moment before, escorted so amiably to the door.

Similarly, as we nearly all recall, children learn to lie to each other as they lie to their teachers, by conditioning themselves to tell teachers, what they guess that teachers wish to hear. Pupils, thus, set as goals of their own present and future education and careers, being careful to say what is likely to be accepted and rewarded, to speak as free from the encumbrance of truthfulness, as such ambitions might appear to demand of them. So, above the doorway to the room where the students' qualifying examinations are held, there often might be emblazoned the motto: "Abandon truth, all ye who enter here!"

In keeping with that motto, teachers, like others, lie in the course of their preying upon those over whom they exert reign. Such teachers would defend their actions by statements of the genre "I was just doing my job," or "Sorry, but that is policy," "That is what is in the textbook," "That is what you have to learn, if you are to pass the examination," "When you finish school, you can make up your own mind, but, for now …," or, simply, "That is the way we teach it here." I recall it all, from all those years, with a certain embittering, and knowledgeable recollection of the fact of fraudulent stuff thrown at me in most of that experience—but, for some rare, blessed exceptions which I cherish to the present day.

Probably, many of you who are adolescents or adults, could report a similar kind of experience, if you were not one of the Americans who usually lie about such matters.

Many common social practices are a reflection of popular acknowledgment of the commonplace fact of such popular habits of customary lying.

For example, few employers assess a job-applicant's resume for the quality of truthfulness, but rather for the desirable or undesirable amount of cleverness to which it attests, and the wish that the applicant, if hired, were likely to be as corrupt in serving the employer's indicated interest, as he or she had been in composing the fiction which the resume contains. "Yes," the hiring officer might confide, "the degree from that university is real, but the education it represents is nearly worthless. Still, the fact that he actually has those degrees covers our backs with the stockholders, in case the fellow turns out to be the bum we suspect he might be. We could say, 'He had the qualifications, but he just didn't work out.'"

Similarly, when an executive is being maneuvered out of the firm, he will be damned with such expressions of faint praise as, "John is to be praised for having done an excellent job, which now prepares the way for obvious improvements."

Similarly, many of the laws which you believe were enacted by our Congress, are lies, in effect. For example, are you so credulous as to believe, that the passage of a law necessarily represents the "intent of Congress"? Do you not know the frequency with which the essential motive for the passing of a particular law was, predominantly, the Congress's intent to recess?

That is not the end of that fraud in law-making practice. Since the so-called "democratic reform" of the Committee structures of the U.S. Congress during the 1970s, there was a directly resulting increase of technical incompetence in the kinds of pieces of legislation emitted from the committees. The conflicts in interpretation of outstanding statute and related policy so clumsily generated, relinquished the responsibility for sorting out those legal conflicts to committees in the Executive Branch's bureaucracy, with the effect that the enforced intent of the legislation, was transformed into what the latter bureaucrats had concocted. So, with the complicity of the courts, intentions which were contrary to the conscious intent of the relevant legislators, became enforced, by authority of the compliant Federal Court, as the official version of "the intent of Congress."

You should be even more shocked by the related kinds of recent trends in decisions respecting the intent of the U.S. Constitution itself, by majorities of the U.S. Supreme Court. Any literate adult who reads the constitutional law upon which our Federal Republic's legal existence depends, the 1776 Declaration of Independence and the 1789 Preamble of the Federal Constitution, can know with certainty that the current, Rehnquist-Scalia majority of the Supreme Court has plainly and solemnly lied, repeatedly and outrageously, against the most crucial point of law in both the Declaration of Independence and the Constitution.

Up to now, I had not mentioned the worst habitual liars of all, the popular mass news media.

"I know that the Moon is made of green cheese."

"That's not true!"

"Are you questioning my sincerity?!"

In everyday life, it is often worse than that.

For example, credulous or simply illiterate citizens attribute great authority to so-called "eyewitness testimony."

Often, good study of circumstantial evidence proves that the eyewitness has either lied, or was simply incompetent to state, as eyewitness, evidence which was, in reality, the kind of conclusion which he, or she had asserted to be the sworn truth of the matter. Or, often, the witness has lied outrightly, but the onlookers declare, still today, that that testimony must be respected, because the witness claimed to have observed with his or her senses, and because foolish onlookers, still today, choose to believe that the witness appears to be, or was described by the judge as sincere. After all, why should typical jurors not tend to sympathize with the species of such liars; are they not often brought up, at home, in schools, and elsewhere, to be the same kinds of liars themselves?

For example, "Experience teaches us!" were, in effect, often the last words of the legendary lemming who then plunged to his death off the cliff.

In each general election, majorities of voters display impassioned confidence in the clown they will come to

Francisco Goya, Los Caprichos*: "Might not the pupil know more?"*

despise by the time the next election comes around. The lout they choose next, to replace the one they have come to despise, is often as bad or worse than the donkey they are about to kick out of office. Worse, often, especially of late, the effect of the citizens' voting, is to chuck out a decent political figure, in momentary preference for someone whom they will have good reason to hate soon enough. Indeed, these days, the majority among those who choose to vote, must be seen, on performance, as never to have learned much worth knowing from their own past experience in voting.

To sum up these points of illustration, add the following.

The typical American will swallow one kind of poison, or another, compulsively, daily, if he, or she believes that experience has taught confidence in that particular brand-name. Indeed, today, we have entered a schizophrenic age of popular illiteracy, in which people wear brand names, in that very large print best suited to the needs of illiterates, on their backs and shirt-fronts, and they mouth brand-names and slogans as if their attention were focussed upon the sensation of fondling those mere phrases with their wet mouths.

In point of fact, in these lunatic times of such mean-spirited pranks as rampant mergers and acquisitions, privatization, and out-sourcing, today's product bearing yesterday's name, may turn out to be, not a horse of a different color, but perhaps an object better suited for use by some yet unknown species, a product selected not for what it is, but for the way the mere brand-name it bears, tastes in the sucker's mouth.

That brings us directly into the provinces of Classical artistic composition. Given the evidence of how widespread the popular forms of lying have become, how do we know what the truth is, and where the evidence may be found on which truthful knowledge depends? Knowledge of how to vote, for example.

Having thus illustrated a point, let me present you now with a generalization whose accuracy I shall unveil to you, step by step, as we proceed together with the following sections of this present report.

Unmaking the World's Worst Mistakes

The principle underlying all competent composition and performance of what is known as Classical tragedy, is based upon the historical evidence it reflects. That principle is, that, in real life off stage, entire cultures, excepting those destroyed by natural causes beyond man's present ability to control, have been usually destroyed by the fatal defects inhering within that prevailing popular culture itself, as the U.S., as a nation, is being destroyed, like the ancient pagan Rome of the popular arena games, by no single factor as weighty as the effect of what is called "popular entertainment" today.

One of the most important lessons of the history of European civilization, is that, throughout that history, the entertainment associated with the theater, has been among the most influential forces, for good, or for evil, in shaping the evolution and consequent fate of that culture as a whole. In this report, I show why that is the case.

In all great Classical tragedy, for example, from Aeschylus and Sophocles, through Shakespeare and Schiller, the tragic failure of the relevant leading figure, such as Shakespeare's Hamlet, or the notorious Oedipus, has been his or her failure to change, willfully and radically, that destiny of a people which custom and related existing institutions of popular influence have brought upon it. So speaks the voice of Shakespeare, through one of his surviving characters, in the closing moments of Hamlet (see box).

The greatest crimes of political leaders, and comparable figures, are usually not their violation of custom, but their failure to violate custom in the manner specifically needed to prevent a people from plunging themselves, and their posterity alike, into some terrible calamity. Thus, the chief cause of the tragedy of nations and cultures, is not that they violated custom or popular opinion, but that they continued to bow to the authority of these precedents and other habits much too long.

"Popular entertainment" in the United States today: professional wrestling.

So, the United States today, is being destroyed politically from within, chiefly by a trend in custom and popular opinion which has been induced by the impact of the combined introduction of the Nixon "Southern Strategy," and Nixon's embrace of the dogma of simple-minded Professor Milton Friedman, about three and a half decades ago.

All great Classical tragedy is based on a case either from actual history, or from popular mythology, in which the destruction of a nation or culture has been brought about by its own accustomed ways.[4] To address this danger from within, the European civilization which emerged in Greece about 2,500 or more years ago, adopted the theatrical performances of the Classical form of tragedy, as an indispensable instrument for examining the dangers inhering in currently accepted customs. Thus, the Homeric epics supplied themes for what emerged as the Classical Greek tragedy of such as Aeschylus and Sophocles. The Classical Greek theater emerged as a more effective way of uplifting the conscience of the citizenry of Athens for this purpose.

The modern Classical tragedy, as it evolved upwards through the efficiently connected work of Marlowe, Shakespeare, Lessing, and Schiller, was a higher form than modern Europe found in those precedents, as from ancient Athens, upon whose foundation the modern form was built.

The method, developed for that purpose, as expressed, and required by the composition and performance of Classical tragedy, is a very definite, readily described, and fairly readily demonstrated one. If the principle could not be demonstrated so, then the theater-goer would never have been moved by well-performed Classical tragedy, as Schiller, for example, the central intellectual figure of the Prussian reformers' national liberation insurgency, moved the German people of his time in a more powerful and revolutionary way than any nation's audiences then or later, through, chiefly, his poetry and plays. Every successful performance of a great Classical tragedy, moves an audience, not because that audience has been deceived, as by a tempting illusion, but, rather, precisely because the audience is led to recognize the efficient principle by means of which they are moved.

People who have failed to understand the basic principle of composing and performing Classical drama, nonetheless tend to suffer the delusion, that the secret of that medium's success lies in the creation of illusion. Unfortunately, just such illiterate nonsense, is the basis for most of what is commonly classed as "Hollywood

---

4. In other words, that dangerous, confessed lunatic, irrational custom, called in German by such Kantian and Hegelian names as *Weltgeist*, *Zeitgeist*, and *Volksgeist*.

> *"Now turn directly, to view the famous Act Three soliloquy of the character Hamlet from the standpoint of negation."*

Hamlet:_ To be, or not to be,—that is the question:
Whether 'tis nobler in the mind to suffer
The slings and arrows of outrageous fortune,
Or, to take arms against a sea of troubles,
And by opposing end them? To die;—to sleep;
No more; and by a sleep, to say we end
The heartaches and the thousand natural shocks
That flesh is heir to: 'tis a consummation
Devoutly to be wished. To die;—to sleep;
To sleep! Perchance to dream! Ay, there's the rub;
For in that sleep of death, what dreams may come,
When we have shuffled off this mortal coil,
Must give us pause. There's the respect
That makes calamity of so long life;
For who would bear the whips and scorns of time,
The oppressor's wrong, the proud man's contumely,
The pangs of despised love, the law's delay,
The insolence of office, and the spurns
That patient merit of the unworthy takes,
When he himself might his quietus make
With a bare bodkin? Who would fardels bear,
To grunt and sweat under a weary life,
But that the dread of something after death,—
The undiscover'd country, from whose bourn
No traveller returns,—puzzles the will,
And makes us rather bear those ills we have
Than fly to others that we know not of?
Thus conscience does make cowards of us all,
And thus the native hue of resolution
Is sicklied o'er with the pale cast of thought,
And enterprises of great pith and moment,

With this regard, their currents turn awry,
And lose the name of action.

> *"Turn to the closing scene of that entire play, and contrast the lines spoken by Fortinbras to the alternative, the proposed prompt reenactment of the tragedy before taking further action, posed in the same location."*

Horatio: Give order that these bodies
High on a stage be placed to the view;
And let me speak to the yet unknowing world
How these things came about: so shall you hear
Of carnal, bloody, and unnatural acts;
Of accidental judgments, casual slaughters;
Of deaths put on by cunning and forc'd cause;
And in this upshot, purposes mistook
Fall'n on the inventors' heads: all this can I
Truly deliver.

Fortinbras: Let us haste to hear it,
And call the noblest to the audience.
For me, with sorrow I embrace my fortune:
I have some rights of memory in this kingdom
Which now to claim my vantage doth invite me.

Horatio: Of that I shall have also cause to speak,
And from his mouth, whose voice will draw on more:
But let this same be presently performed,
Even while men's minds are wild, lest more mischance
On plots and errors happen.

Fortinbras: Let four captains
Bear Hamlet like a soldier to the stage....
The soldier's music and the rites of war
Speak loudly for him....

productions" today. As we might observe by studying the declaration of the actor playing Chorus, directly to the assembled audience, in the opening of Shakespeare's **King Henry V**, no illusion is intended. Rather, the principle of the stage encountered in the tragedies, for example, of Shakespeare and Schiller, is the Socratic principle of truth, as that principle was first explicitly and rigorously defined for science by Plato, in his dialogues.

I explain the difference.

The art of illusion, or "magic," is to play a trick on the audience's senses, to no other immediate purpose, than to make things appear to sense-certainty as what they are not. For example: cheap-shot sensationalism, as typified by such experiences as Hollywood-style "science fiction" nonsense, and some recent campaigns of leading Presidential candidates.

In contrast to that, the Classical stage copies Classical poetry, and the Homeric epics, in crafting an image of what the audience comes to recognize as the efficient factors, intangible to the senses as such, which are shaping the real outcome of the events presented. To accomplish this, the playwright and performers rely on methods on which that ability depends, to reconstruct the image of such factors on a certain kind of stage which is erected only inside the mind of each member of the audience, that done without the aid of any of the tricks consistent with the definition of illusion.

Thus, Chorus tells the audience to use their imagination, as I shall explain, a bit later, what the term "imagination" should be understood to mean. The play does nothing to lure the members of the audience into the grip of illusions.

For example, Chorus explicitly warns them against being lured into il-

"The European civilization which emerged in Greece about 2,500 or more years ago, adopted the theatrical performances of the Classical form of tragedy, as an indispensable instrument for examining the dangers inhering in currently accepted customs." Here: a Greek amphitheater.

lusions not intended by their vision and hearing of the performance of that play. Shakespeare does not pretend to put the actual events on stage, as an illusionist would pretend to do. Shakespeare uses the stage to focus the audience's attention on what is happening to the minds, and in the interactions among, the characters abstracted from the real-life, off-stage reality to which the drama makes reference.

This method of Shakespeare's and Schiller's stage, as implied by Chorus' address to the audience, is derived from the allegory of Plato's Cave. Once this point is made clear to you, you will have overcome the biggest hurdle which you must overcome to understand what your exposure to entertainment does, or does not do, to and for you. That explanation finds its root, not in the classroom's course in literary criticism, but in the hard reality of physical science.

As all literate adults know, the difference between the relationship to nature by mankind, and that of any lower animal species, lies in the ability, unique to the individual human mind, of discovering experimentally validatable discoveries of universal physical principles. By means of these discoveries, and of the technologies

derived from them, the individual human mind is enabled to cause a willful and qualitative increase in the so-called "ecological potential" which is characteristic of the entire human species, something which no animal species can duplicate.

That said, we zero-in on the core of the matter at hand. Now ask yourself the question, can you see a universal physical principle with your eyes? Can you identify such a principle itself as in any way an object of the senses?

By a validated discovery of a universal physical principle, we mean something which can not be seen, heard, smelled, or touched by organs of the senses, but, an idea, as Plato defines ideas, by means of which, man's power to exist, in and over the universe, is measurably increased. Thus, such principles are physically efficient causes of definite, tangible kinds of changes in our relationship to nature. These changes are measurable effects, and, thus, to be regarded as "hard and tangible" realities, but the efficient causes for those changes, the principles themselves, those *ideas*, are not the kinds of objects which, as themselves, can be detected directly by the senses.

KING HENRY V.

Act IV. Sc. 7.

Piece out our imperfections with your thoughts:
Into a thousand parts divide one man,
And make imaginary puissance;
Think, when we talk of horses, that you see them
Printing their proud hoof i'the receiving earth;
For 'tis your thoughts that now must deck our kings,
Carry them here and there; jumping o'er times,
Turning the accomplishment of many years
Into an hour-glass: for the which supply,
Admit me chorus to this history;
Who, prologue-like, your humble patience pray,
Gently to hear, kindly to judge, our play.

This is the leading point made by the allegory of Plato's Cave. That, as I shall make the point clearer below, is the conception of ideas, on which all successful composition and performance of Classical tragedy depends, absolutely, for its successful effect upon the audience. The point to which this report as a whole is addressed, is to show you that that same principle of composition and performance of Classical tragedy, should be the basis for the way in which you organize your mind for your discussion of not only the experimentally validated discovery of universal physical principles, but also any other serious issue of policy-making, with the person with whom you chance to discuss such a matter, even in a relatively brief exchange at a street-corner.

At this point, from this point in the present report, onwards, I shall now walk you, first, through the steps by which a validatable form of discovery of a universal physical principle is made. After that, I shall show you how that same principle of scientific thinking, governs the way in which the relationship between Classical drama and the living audience functions. In either science, or Classical art, what I shall thus describe to you, is exactly what transpires in every case such a validatable discovery in science has occurred.

This principle I now, once again, set before you, is *the principle of what is known as "geometry of position," as it is not only the fact in known cases; more important, it is the only way in which such a discovery could be made*. Once we have examined the evidence for the case of the discovery of universal physical principles, we shall examine other kinds of universal principles which are generated, as known and provable ideas, by the same kinds of mental activity, and discourse among persons, used for the successful discovery and communication of validated universal physical principles.

Our practical aim in focussing your attention on those principles of mental life which are indispensable, both to scientific progress, and for overcoming the cultural failures of certain cultures, is to demonstrate to you those methods which history has shown to be indispensable for unmaking the present world's worst mistakes.

2. What Are Ideas?

The relevant, functional relationship between the Classical drama on stage and the individual mind of the member of the audience, is the immediate topic on which to focus attention now. Once that connection is made clear, one might hope that the reader would recognize that the relationship of a speaker to his friend or acquaintance, in the proper art of truthful conversation, as in discussing any serious topic, even on a street-corner, is a replication of the same kind of situation existing between the drama and the audience in a Classical theatrical performance.

In this course of completing this report, I shall come to the point that I am prepared to show, that the person speaking on that street-corner, is adopting the role of the playwright or actor, and, for that instant, the hearer is playing the part of the member of the audience. If the other responds in kind, the ensuing conversation is embarked on the beginning of what we might hope will become a real-life re-enactment of the principle of Plato's Socratic dialogues.

Such a relationship among persons discussing what I have identified as *ideas*—Platonic ideas, and facts pertaining to them, is the method of discourse indispensable for reaching those forms of agreement which may be rightly regarded and used *as being truthful*. It is in that specific sense, that we may rightly speak of truth as a quality most naturally specific to the media of Classical art-forms. Granted, there is truthfulness required of physical science, but that quality of truthfulness, when it is found there, as the opposite is met in the currently prevalent popular practice of lying in the U.S. today, is a matter of social relations. The quality of truthfulness shared with scientific knowledge, is realized through those same social processes which are the immediate subject-matter of Classical art-forms as such.

Truthfulness is a quality of *ideas*, as Plato's Socratic method demonstrates the reality of *ideas*. Classical art's source of authority for statecraft, is that it is specifically the medium most appropriate for adducing the relative truthfulness of the ideas by which a nation or culture chooses to rule its affairs.

In the alternative, there is no truthfulness in any other place than the domain of *ideas* so defined. Any literal interpretation of mere sense-impressions as such, is, by nature, an illusion, a deception, and therefore a lie. The question of truthfulness, is not a matter of sense-certainty; it lies entirely within the bounds of the value we place upon ideas, as the allegory of Plato's Cave distinguishes between the falseness of the mere shadows cast upon the wall of a firelit cave, and the beings and actions which are naturally misrepresented by a literal reading of those mere shadows which we call sense-certainties.

Once that equivalence of Classical theater and ordinary modes of serious discussion of ideas, is recognized, then, I expect the reader to recognize the fact, that we should regard Classical theater as Friedrich Schiller did, as the medium through which a people can understand the way in which audiences can learn to discuss important issues in the course of everyday life. This kind of attitude and practice within the population as a citizenry, is what we must now establish as the method of deliberation on which the citizens of our republic must rely, more and more, in choosing the ideas and related policies by which that republic shall be self-governed.

On that account, the pivot of the pertinent argument which I must summarize for you at this point, is also supplied in a somewhat different context, in a just recently published report, "The Lesson of the Cole Incident," published in the November 10, 2000 edition of the English-language, political intelligence news-weekly, the **Executive Intelligence Review**. The argument is presented there in the portion of that feature located on pages 43-48, under the included subheadings of "The Scientific Basis for Recovery" and "Geometry of Position."

My purpose here and now, is to identify a principle, a principle called by such names as "*Analysis Situs*" or "geometry of position," as the common basis for all scientific discovery and for the relationship between the Classical tragedy on stage and the mind of the audience. The object of that clarification, is to point out to you how the presently almost unknown, virtually lost art of competent practice of politics, actually works. My purpose in that, is to make clear to you that this is something which you as a citizen, can master with a reasonable amount of effort, as aided by the acquired habit of practice of relevant discussion among selected representatives of your circles of friends and acquaintances.

The matter to be addressed, is introduced most readily by reference to the characteristic folly of that classroom, in which today's still conventional view of so-called Euclidean geometry is accepted, wrongly, as a standard of truthfulness.

The specific lie which permeates blind faith in such a classroom geometry, is the assumption, premised on always deceptive sense-certainty, both that space, in three assumed directions of forward-backward, sideways, and up-down, is simply extended infinitely, and that time is simply extended, similarly, in a forward-backward sense of direction. This lie is expressed typically by the notion that relations of matter in space and time are to be defined, in their most elementary terms, by the notion of action at a distance, as that fraudulent view is associated with such names as Galileo, Descartes, and Newton.

The system traditionally taught in classrooms as "Euclidean geometry," expressed these ivory-tower delusions of infantile sense-certainty. It thus insisted, respecting space, time, and matter, on mimicking an Aristotelean form, and interpretation of definitions, axioms, and postulates. These assumptions, which I have just broadly described, respecting space, time, and matter, were falsely asserted to be the standpoint from which the apparent physical evidence of our senses was to be described, and interpreted. Such is what is fairly described as "the ivory-tower mentality" commonly polluting, still today, the generally accepted, classroom teaching of, and credulous students' underlying beliefs concerning mathematical physics.

This was the issue on which the founder of modern astrophysics, Johannes Kepler, demonstrated the intrinsic incompetence of the methods previously employed for astronomy, by Claudius Ptolemy, Copernicus, and Tycho Brahe—and, later, by Galileo. Two discoveries dated chiefly to the beginning of the Seventeenth Century, illustrate a point which is of crucial importance for knowing how the Classical theater's relationship to the audience functions.

The first such example, is the case of Kepler's tracking the evidence that the Mars orbit is elliptical, to define a universal lawfulness of the organization of the Solar System as a whole.[5] The second, is the demonstration, first by the great Fermat, of the evidence showing that least time, rather than shortest distance, was the efficient principle governing the propagation of light.[6]

In both of the latter instances, the method employed was typical of most of the so-called crucial demonstrations of a discovered scientific principle of physical science. It is the implications of that method of demonstration, on which I ask you to focus your attention in connection with the matter of Classical drama.

The way in which these discoveries were defined, was, in the first approximation, by showing that the interpretation of the observed phenomena led to an obvious absurdity, as long as the attempt persisted, to represent these patterns according to what today's generally accepted classroom teaching of elementary mathematical physics, insists is the required method of representation of the evidence.

In other words, imagine a case, in which mathematical statement "A," is both a truthful representation of the apparent empirical evidence, and also one consistent with such "Euclidean" mathematical schemes. Then, compare that with a case, in which the same collection of empirical evidence produces a second statement, "B," also in the same form, which, in effect, is violently in contradiction with the conclusions implied by the first statement, "A." The result is, that since both statements are consistent, in origin, with the system, and, yet, both imply results which violate that system, the conjunction of the two statements creates a condition which is a *negation* of the system from which the two statements are ostensibly derived. In other words, what is called an *ontological paradox*. Hereinafter, I employ the term "negation" in no different sense than that.

In the case of situating the added evidence, respecting the elliptical form of the Mars orbit, Kepler recognized that this led to contradictions within the previously interpreted empirical evidence. These contradictions warned Kepler, that we must step outside the attempt to explain orbits by simply connecting the dots among observed positions, and seek out a physical principle, outside the assumptions of Euclidean geometry. The evidence today, shows that Kepler was right, and that all of those upholding the commonly accepted empiricist and related views, are false to reality.

---

5. Tennenbaum, Director, et al. "How Gauss Determined the Orbit of Ceres," **Fidelio**, Summer, 1998.

---

6. The reference is to two letters in which Pierre Fermat announced (in 1662) his discovery that light always propagates itself by a principle of least time. The letters, to de la Chambre, are found in French in **Oeuvres de Fermat**, Vol. II, p. 354 and p. 457.

The same kind of approach was employed by Fermat, to show that the refraction of light was governed by a principle described, in first approximation, as "least time," rather than "shortest distance." The continuation of that investigation by Huyghens, Leibniz, et al., led into the modern, relativistic hyper-geometries of Carl Gauss and Bernhard Riemann, from which all "Euclidean" and other "ivory tower" sets of definitions, axioms, and postulates are excluded, and only, as Riemann was first to specify publicly, experimentally validated discoveries of universal physical principles are accepted as having the authority formerly, wrongfully, attributed to arbitrary, *aprioristic* axioms.

This method in modern physical science can be shown, conclusively, to be anticipated in the work of Plato and others. It is also inherent in the method of modern experimental science, as that body of science was founded by Cardinal Nicholas of Cusa during the mid-Fifteenth Century, and by such prominent students and followers of Cusa as Leonardo da Vinci. Kepler, for example, relied heavily, and explicitly, upon such aspects of the work of Cusa and Leonardo, and also Plato, in his discovery and initial development of modern astrophysics. However, it is from the starting-point of the crisis in the Seventeenth and Eighteenth Centuries' physical science, which crisis Kepler's work introduced to those centuries, that the sweep of development of modern physical science has unfolded to date.

The differences between the ancient Greek forms of Classical tragedy, and the development by Marlowe, Shakespeare, Lessing, and Schiller, has a specific quality of distinction which belongs to the period of crisis, erupting during the Sixteenth Century, following the revolution in ideas which had erupted during the previous, Fifteenth-Century Renaissance. The specific form in which modern Classical art, and modern science developed, have that common history, and correspondingly distinct, common characteristics.

However, those references to scientific matters here, are introduced here for the limited purpose of showing how the same principles of discovery, function as the essentially determining characteristic of Classical art-forms in general, and the Classical tragedy's relationship to its audiences, in particular.

The common feature of science and art, on which our attention is focussed, is the implications of the notion called "geometry of position." To bridge that relationship between science and art, I turn to the case of Classical musical composition, which, as I shall show, is based on exactly those principles which connect the Classical drama to the mind of the member of the audience.

The Art of The Fugue

In his **The Art of the Fugue**, the founder of the method of modern Classical musical composition, Johann Sebastian Bach, presented an ordered series of pedagogical exercises, which, in fact, summarize the process of development visibly traceable in his life's work up to the close of his life in 1750. This principle so presented there, is otherwise typified earlier by his **A Musical Offering**.[7] It was the latter composition, intensively studied, ostensibly from a time beginning about 1782, by Wolfgang Mozart, which led Mozart to combine what he had learned from both Josef Haydn[8] and Bach, to effect that revolution in the method of composing Classical polyphony, which became known by such names as the *Classical thorough-composition* of such composers as Mozart, the later Haydn, Beethoven, Schubert, Mendelssohn, Schumann, and Brahms. It is that notion of thorough-composition, which I reference here, to demonstrate the relationship between an adequate performance of Classical tragedy and the audience.

This principle, as identified explicitly by Bach in his **The Art of the Fugue**, is a direct reflection of the method exhibited by the referenced work of Kepler and Fermat, et al. Accordingly, to compose such Classical music, or to derive a corresponding quality of song from such a musical idea, the following elementary steps must be completed.

State an interval, or a series of intervals of three tones in a well-tempered ordering of the musical scale, referenced at virtually C=256. Next, add a complementary statement, inverting some of the order in the series of intervals of the first statement. Do this in such a way,

7. See EIR, June 23, 2000, pp. 5-53, for two-days' presentations of this principle of Bach's **A Musical Offering** and related works, at a conference of the Schiller Institute in Bad Schwalbach, Germany, May 27-28, 2000.

8. Compare Haydn's "Russian Quartets," Opus 33, with Mozart's "Haydn Quartets," K. 387, 421, 428, 458, 464, and 465. See reprint of Lyndon H. LaRouche, Jr., "Mozart's 1782-1786 Revolution in Music," **EIR**, Vol. 44, No. 4, Jan. 27, 2017.

Beethoven's Application of the Bach-Haydn-Mozart Principle of Thorough-Composition

Ludwig van Beethoven's Mass in C, Op. 86 is a masterpiece in the use of inversion of complementary statements, each of which appear "nominally" in the same mode, but whose juxtaposition, as LaRouche puts it, "leads inevitably, through development through a series of quasi-dissonances of a type associated with the notion of Lydian intervals."

In the opening "Kyrie" movement, Beethoven states the single interval of a rising fourth. In the complementary statement which immediately follows, he then inverts this into a descending fourth:

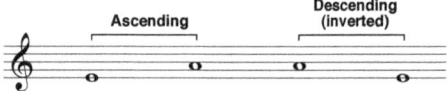

These two intervals are stated in two different voices, each with its own characteristic vocal register-shift. In the first statement, the soprano voice shifts vocal registers across the interval, from the low "chest" register, to the middle register; whereas the second interval is stated by the alto section, composed of contraltos and mezzosopranos, all of whom remain in the middle register throughout. The lack of a register-shift in the alto voice sets up a creative tension that is only resolved at the movement's conclusion.

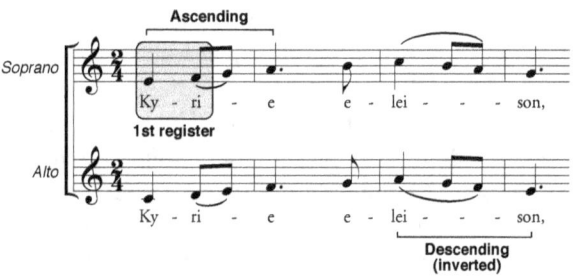

Throughout the movement, these two intervals are repeatedly juxtaposed and altered, generating multiple quasi-dissonances, especially with counterpositions of the "nominal" C Major scale, to the major scale that is based on the lowest note of the opening interval—E Major—thereby implying a complex of Lydian-type relationships to the original C Major.

The movement culminates in the jarring, simultaneous juxtaposition of both the rising interval, this time in the tenor voice, and an altered version of the falling interval, sung by the altos, but this time descending into the mezzosoprano's chest register, thereby satisfying the tension created at the outset.

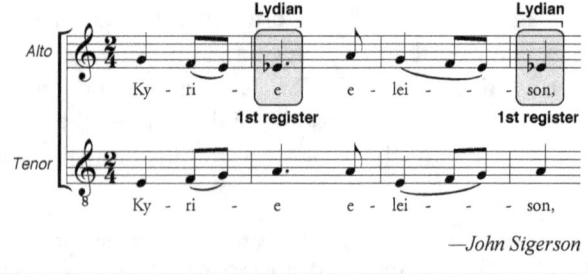

—John Sigerson

that, in an example of first approximation, each statement is derived from the same implied key, but the juxtaposition of this leads inevitably, through development, through a series of quasi-dissonances of a type associated with the notion of Lydian intervals (**Figure 1**). Bach's **A Musical Offering** is a model example of this. Mozart's recapitulation of that work of Bach, in his K.475 keyboard **Fantasy**, summarily identifies that revolutionary step by Mozart, on which all Classical thorough-composition thereafter depended for its precedent (**Figure 2**).

See this as echoing the examples of the previously referenced, similar conception by Kepler and Fermat earlier. The generation of a musical dissonance, in that fashion, produces an effect which is identical in form and implication to the cases of the paradoxes posed by Kepler and Fermat, respectively, in the physical-science examples. In musical terms, inversions crafted to produce that effect, are recognized as dissonances, because, on the condition that the dissonances are resolved within the completed composition, they create transcendental qualities of musical keys, beyond the 24-key major-minor domain, just as discovered universal physical principles lie beyond and above the bounds of the axiomatic system into which such paradoxes are introduced.

In that sense, such paradoxical juxtapositions, such as those generated by musical, contrapuntal inversion, negate the system into which they are introduced, just as Kepler's and Fermat's discoveries *negate* the system of assumptions into which they are introduced. It is in this sense, and only this sense, that, as I have said above, I employ the term *negation* hereinafter. Negation signifies a paradox which obliges us to find reality in principles which exist outside a referenced system of axiomatic-like assumptions. Such paradoxes thus *negate* the referenced system of axiomatic-like assumptions.

Now, turn directly, to view the famous Act Three soliloquy of the character Hamlet from the standpoint of negation. The statement and its inversion, for this case, are "To be," conjoined to "or, not to be." Try hearing someone recite that soliloquy, even some celebrated recorded performance by a famous actor, and then explain to the person next to you, exactly, why the usual actor who delivered that recitation does not know what he is talking about!

Read the soliloquy. Identify the way in which the actor Shakespeare would have intended to play Hamlet, and would have delivered that soliloquy. I shall give you a hint as to how to discover what that would be. Turn to the closing scene of that entire play, and contrast the lines spoken by Fortinbras, to the alternative: the proposed prompt re-enactment of the tragedy before taking further action, posed in the same location (see box).

For an easy comparison, reference the dialogue on principles of law, among Socrates, Thrasymachus, and Glaucon, in Plato's **Republic**.[9] There, Socrates' use of the same principle of *agapē* set forth in Paul's **I Corinthians** 13, appears as a higher standpoint from which the negation posed among Socrates, Thrasymachus, and Glaucon, is overcome through the discovery of a relevant higher principle. In Shakespeare's **Hamlet**, by contrast, it is the negation of Hamlet's folly, as Hamlet states his intent to doom both himself and the Kingdom of Denmark, by his refusal to abandon his customary, "macho's" mode of swashbuckling conduct, which is the higher principle adduced by the audience. In Classical thorough-composition, as in the conclusion of the fourth song of Brahms' **Four Serious Songs**, it is Brahms' concluding treatment of the *agapē* of **I Corinthians** 13, which is the subject of the kind of higher resolution typical of the poetic settings typical of Mozart, Beethoven, Schubert, Brahms et al.

So, we have thus now touched here upon the essence of the subject of the modern Classical tragedy. However, there is a second principle to be examined, without which the art of successful forms of composition and performance of Classical music, poetry, and tragedy, could not be competently accomplished, or understood. The issue is typified by considering the function of musicality in composing that poem without words, otherwise called a "song without words," on which the greatest writings in poetry, are to be understood, as Friedrich Schiller insisted to a Goethe who was reluctant to acknowledge that higher plane of musicality in poetry, shown in the song compositions of Mozart, Beethoven, Schubert, and, implicitly, also, the later cases of Schumann and Brahms.

FIGURE 2
Mozart's K. 475 Recapitulation of Bach's *A Musical Offering*

The opening statement of J.S. Bach's A Musical Offering, *showing the Lydian interval evoked between the C of the first half of the statement, and the F-sharp, on the first stressed beat of the second half.*

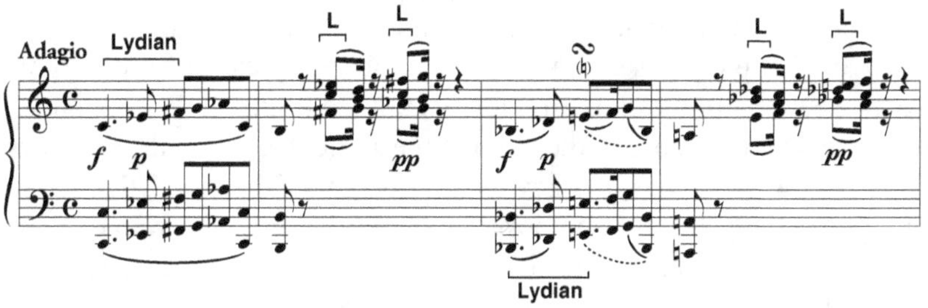

In his Fantasy for Piano, K. 475, Mozart condenses Bach's conception into a brief, but extremely intense statement, incorporating the Lydian interval into the very first measure.

3. Songs Without Words

Relatively illiterate people, who have yet to gain a competent sense of artistry, usually make the terrible blunder, of assuming, falsely, that the meaning of a Classical poem is to be found primarily, and originally, in the literal text of the poem. Unfortunately, such misguided fellows often recite and threaten to ruin the reputation of such poetry, in just that awful, putting-off, unbeautiful, often bombastic way.

On this account, I find most useful a statement by the now famous baritone, Dietrich Fischer-Dieskau, sometime youthful collaborator of the famous director Wilhelm Furtwängler, and early hailed by some, including me, during the early 1950s, as the prospective successor to Heinrich Schlusnus. I refer to a statement which Fischer-Dieskau has made in a recently broadcast observation on the subject of language, music, and poetry, to which I attach extraordinary importance on account of the issue which I have just posed.[10] It were a

9. In Plato's dialogue, "The Republic—(On Justice)," Book 1, **Plato**, Loeb Classical Library (Cambridge, Mass.: Harvard University Press, 1975).

10. Baritone Fischer-Dieskau's remarks on language, poetry, and Lied were seen originally on German and French television, in a documentary film entitled, "Dietrich Fischer-Dieskau: La Voix de l'âme. Geburtstag" ("Birthday Tribute to Dietrich Fischer-Dieskau: The Voice of the Soul").

proper undertaking of our best musical artists today, the Classical singers most notably, to look at Fischer-Dieskau's observation as I do. The same quality is exhibited in the related work, in the German repertoire in particular, of a recently deceased dear friend, Gertrude Pitzinger,[11] as in the best among others. There is, for reasons I shall indicate, a great profit for art specifically, and for humanity in general, in pursuing that line of investigation.

As I shall now indicate, this matter of musicality of a Classical poem, as that principle of poetry must, contrary to the awful mannerisms of the late Sir Lawrence Olivier, inform the playwright and performing artist, is crucial for recognizing the manner in which a successful performance of Shakespeare, for example, reaches into the deepest, most intimate region of both the cognitive powers and passions of the mind of the audience. It is also, in the same way, the key to recognition of the principle underlying the composition of the greatest Classical instrumental compositions, and to the relationship between the singers and the chorus of instrumental voices in Classical musical compositions generally.

Return to the observations which I made, above, on the function of the principle of inversion expressed in the referenced compositions by Bach and Mozart.

Among the rules for development of a long-lasting and beautiful development of the human singing voice, is obedience to the combined, and, actually, interdependent standards set by both the Florentine species of so-called *bel canto* development and use of the human singing voice, and the strictly well-tempered set of singing-voice (Keplerian, astrophysical-like) *orbits* (tonalities) defined by J.S. Bach's method in polyphonic counterpoint. Although such capabilities of the best singers require a cultivation of natural gifts, the gifts so cultivated, are a pre-existing disposition of not only the human singing-voice, and, also, speaking voice, apparatus, but are, as is often, most unfortunately, overlooked, also innate qualities of the human mental processes, the impassioned attributes of cognition most notably.

It is upon these considerations that the principles of Classical forms of poetic composition depend, both for their expression, and for the comprehension of the hearer.

---

11. Her performance of the Schumann Frauenliebe and of the Brahms Vier Ernste Gesänge, are notable examples.

The consequence of those considerations which has the most direct bearing upon the subject-matter of this report as a whole, is the following.

In the case of the Classical song, as in the musical setting of Classical poem, we are confronted with two functionally distinct kinds of musical orderings. One ordering, is that determined by the *bel canto*-specific vocalization of the poetry itself. The other ordering, is that determined according to the principles of composition defined by well-tempered contrapuntal thorough-composition.

That is to say, on the first account, that, in each language, or its dialectal variant, a distinct relative intonation is associated with the distinction of one vowel from another. This is coupled with the impact of the consonants. And, so on and so forth. In the attempt at a literal rendering of a poem by a speaker, the tendency of literate speakers, of which admittedly few emerge from our secondary and university education of recent decades, is to follow the musical line of the language's or dialect's so-called natural prosody, its seemingly natural musical expression. That is to say, the poem is read by the literate speaker of that language, as a musical score.

This was, speaking in relative terms, the view expressed by Goethe and his factional ally Reichardt, respecting the musical setting of Goethe's own poetry. Hearing the settings of poetry by Reichardt, illustrates Goethe's standpoint in this matter. Schiller disagreed, as did Wolfgang Mozart, Beethoven, and Franz Schubert. The differences between the treatment of Goethe's poetry, the one by Reichardt, the other by Mozart, Beethoven, and Schubert, confronts us with the relevant illustration of the issue to be considered here.

Simply stated, the correct approach to the musicality of Classical poetry, is that of Schiller, as Schiller's argument against Goethe and Reichardt is demonstrated so elegantly in practice by the Goethe settings, and other songs, of Mozart, Beethoven, and Schubert, as also by the songs composed by Schumann and Brahms later. In the examples provided by such composers, it is the standpoint of Bach's well-tempered contrapuntal polyphony which dominates the musical reading of the prosody. *The difference in result, is that the latter approach produces a work in the mode of well-tempered thorough-composition.*

The difference imposed by the application of the contrapuntal idea upon the relatively naive prosodic reading of the poem, is that the musical departures from the simply prosodic reading of the poetic line, must never be arbitrary impositions of the speakers' or singers' opinion, but must have a lawful reason. The point is, that in art, nothing must ever be arbitrary, never as the Romantics and so forth insist upon arbitrary, irrational whims, whims whose claims to art are limited to the presumption that that which is utterly irrational, such as the works of Richard Wagner, is unfathomably mysterious, and therefore incredibly artistic and sexy as well. There must be governing necessity, as there is in science. That governing principle of reason, must be supplied by the governing, underlying role of contrapuntal development, the contrapuntal development derived from the spark of well-tempered thorough-composition.

This latter view of the challenge posed by the musical settings of poetry, forces us to recognize, in the relatively clearest possible way, the kernel of the method by which the noblest compositions and performances in Classical tragedy, such as those of Shakespeare and Schiller, impart a cognitive passion within the audience, like no other works of similar kinds.

This takes us directly to the highest level of the art of politics. It focusses our attention on the way in which a well-performed Classical tragedy generates a certain condition within the mind of the sensitive members of the audience. This effect is essentially of the same character as the effect upon a musically literate audience of a well-delivered Classical musical song, or, for example, a Verdi aria such as the famous monologue from **Simon Boccanegra**, or the aria of the dying Posa in **Don Carlos**, or a well-performed delivery of the hateful soliloquy of Iago, which Verdi added to his earlier setting of Shakespeare's **Othello**. The best singers love such parts from the repertoire, because of the way in which appropriate performance enables the singer to reach deeply into the mind of the individual member of the audience. The audiences love such performances, and regard them as beautiful, on the same account. This is the crucial consideration, thorough-compositional musicality and all, in the effective performance of a great Classical tragedy, such as those of Shakespeare and Schiller.

My intention here, is that you, the reader, should develop at least the rudiments of the ability to touch the inside of the mind of your conversation-partners, in ways consistent with that same principle. This is the quality you should recognize as underlying Plato's composition of his dialogues. This is the principle expressed in practice by the greatest poets, and by, yet once again, the Classical tragedies of Shakespeare and Schiller.

Classical beauty, is not an object at which to look in admiration, or, perhaps, lust. Such beauty is a relationship among persons, a relationship between the cognitive processes of the artist, on the one side, and the cognitive process of the audience, on the other. Only in what humanity has developed as Classical modes of artistry, is such communication efficiently accomplished.

Such art never descends to the banality of mere entertainment. It has a sacred spiritual quality, expressing a quality of the human cognitive processes, by means of which they celebrate and impose that law, that each man and woman is made in the image of the Creator of this universe. Here lies the superior moral authority of great Classical artistic composition and its performance. Here lies the wellspring of that moral authority which, as Shelley has reported, presents poets to us as the true legislators of mankind. Here lies that power in Classical artistic composition, which is never equalled in social authority by any other form of communication.

That said, now focus upon what might be described as the mechanisms, by means of which the Classical tragedy reaches deep into the cognitive processes of the mind of the member of the audience. How is the apparent stress between the two notions of musicality, those of prosody and well-tempering, to be resolved?

How To Compose a Poem

At this point, I must confess. I once did compose Classical poetry, many decades ago. It was a passable product, but that nasty *Zeitgeist* whose satanic grip had claimed to grip my times, forbade such products from disturbing the complacency of rampant current custom. I consoled myself, that I had done enough to grasp the rudiments of such composition, and had gained thereby some of the essential insight which fed into the possibility of the discoveries which I have contributed to the science of physical economy. Among the benefits of that experience, as combined with my apprentice's insight into some of the greatest Classical compositions, I present you now, with what is a reliable summary of the method by which a modern piece of Classical poetry is to be composed. This is an approximation of course, but it is exact and accurate as to matter of the most elementary principles involved.

To compose a Classical poem, one should put the matter of text to one side, at least for a while, and concentrate fully on the most elementary principles of Bach's counterpoint.

On that account, let us assume that you have developed a fertile musical mind, at least to the degree that your thoughts are haunted by an ever-proliferating abundance of those kinds of musical ideas to which I have referred above: statement and inversion, as in the kind of counterpoint which leads potentially to Classical thorough-composition. It is out of what the printer calls the "hell box" of such stereotypical musical elements, that the proper poet, such as a John Keats for English, chooses a musical idea which he or she decides has an ingenious potential relationship to the musicality of a certain fragment of prosodic text.

If that poet has grasped the lesson which my references to the poetic musicality of Schiller, Mozart, and so on, imply, then the contrapuntal idea so chosen, serves as a driving force for the developmental elaboration and resolution of the prosodic element in question. This principle is demonstrated by such an example as Mozart's setting of **Das Veilchen**, and by the alterations in a Goethe poem typical of the musical settings of Mozart, Beethoven, and Schubert, and the sundry song-compositions of Schumann and Brahms. A most intriguing and fruitful connection, is shown by comparing the Heine settings by Schubert with the Heine settings of Schumann.

Under the governance of that kind of partnership between counterpoint and prosody, a good poet, whether adequately aware of this connection or not, will find himself, or herself carried, as on empyreal waves, to the full exposition of the germ-idea of his composition, unfolding as what becomes a satisfactory, completed development of the poem as a whole. To understand this most efficiently, it were sufficient to focus upon the role of a series of Lydian intervals in a short composition such as the Mozart **Ave Verum Corpus**, or his earlier **Abendempfindung**. In effect, the song-setting as performed, is driven by the energy, the passion, of the contrapuntal process, toward its goal of the completion of a perfectly coherent single idea, an idea whose expression requires neither more nor less than what has been composed and performed.

So far, up to this point, I have described the most essential formalities of the business. That much said, turn to the kernel of the matter. How does this all work within the mind of the member of the audience?

Perhaps more than routine familiarity with the Classical song-form is required for this, but, with work, the principle involved can be adduced in an empirical way. In the case of songs in the form of Classical thorough-composition, the idea of "songs without words" comes to the fore in a manner and degree which is, at first, not only astonishing, but stunningly so. Without words, such music, indeed, all Classical thorough-composition, represents a distinct idea, an idea without words. On this account, it seems at least as sensible to put words to music, as music to words. Every truly gifted Classical instrumental performer readily recognizes this certain quality which lies between the notes, the quality which guides the artistically successful performer, and which dooms some technically well-trained others.

The success of such performing between the notes, should be treated as a form of empirical evidence, showing that those qualities of the composer's and performer's minds which enable the Classical performance to reach into the virtual soul of the mind of the audience, are successful precisely because there is a resonance between those aspects of the creative, cognitive processes of both parties.

This should suggest to us, and it can be shown conclusively on solid ground, that the musicality which underlies well-tempered thorough-composition, and such uses of prosody as poetry and the great compositions of Classical tragedy, are essential, or, in other words, indispensable qualities of the power of individual human cognition itself.

In that sense and degree, the person who is unresponsive to Classical modes of composition and performance of poetry, music generally, and tragedy, is an emotional and cognitive illiterate, lacking in the development of an otherwise inborn, natural ability of the human individual, to think and communicate in cognitive, rather than merely deductive modes. Thus, these overtones of such principles of musicality, are inextricably linked to the arts of irony function, metaphor most emphatically. Without a certain literacy of the cognitive powers, on this account, the ability of the individual to see a remedy for a seemingly insoluble paradox, such as that of the Hamlet soliloquy, were impossible. On that account, and exactly that account, an entire people, an entire nation, an entire culture might be doomed to a catastrophe inflicted by its own hand.

The object of the leading personalities of society,

must therefore be to awaken and to address those cognitive qualities of the individual mind, in which the passion required to induce cognitive solutions to paradoxes is aroused by musicality. To make this point transparent, return to the matter of geometry of position.

Closing In On Ideas

In Classical art, ideas have the same geometry as those ideas generated as validated discoveries of universal physical principle. As the case of the elementary idea in well-tempered contrapuntal statement and inversion illustrates the connection, all ideas arise within the human mind, solely by Socratic forms of *negation.*

That is to emphasize, that the type of idea posed by negation does not exist in the explicit elements of the respective parts of the conjunction. It exists, apparently, solely in the gap, the discontinuity which the contradictory feature of the conjunction situates. The idea occurs as a demonstrably efficient solution, existing outside either of the conjoined elements, for the paradox posed by the conjunction. The discovery of an empirically validated universal physical principle, is the archetype of such solutions to such forms of paradox. The point to be emphasized, is that all artistic ideas are of exactly the same form as the discovery of an experimentally validated universal physical principle.

Thus, the conjunction which I have made in the opening paragraph of this report, typifies the way in which a writer or speaker seeks to break through formalities to address the cognitive processes of the mind of the member of the audience. It is right to laugh *together with* Senator Eugene McCarthy in the matter of his readings of poetry. It is right *not to laugh at* Lincoln's readings of Shakespeare to the members of his cabinet. It is therefore silly, to deprecate the role of Classical art in shaping history. Why is this so? That poses a paradox. What is the answer to that paradox?

The purpose of all serious communication, even an exchange on a street-corner, is to bring into play the inner, cognitive processes of the person to whom one is speaking. It is only through the provocation of those cognitive processes, that real paradoxes of real life practice, can be transformed into cognitively generated knowledge of solutions to those problems. No other kinds of solutions to genuine, real-life paradoxes, exist.

The function of the Classical tragedy is to capture the audience's attention from the start, by posing a paradoxical situation, a dramatic form of geometry of position, which admits of no discoverable solution except the generation of a cognitive form of discovery within the mind of the individual member of the audience.

If this address to the audience is successful in achieving that immediate goal, the result is to put the unfolding drama onto the stage of the imagination of the individual member of the audience. The object is to circumvent the potentially fatal error, of the empiricist's or materialist's blundering misapprehension of the shadows projected upon the wall of Plato's fire-lit Cave. The problem so defined by the theater, is the need to get the mind of the audience to shift its focus from a literal interpretation of the physical stage as such, the walls of the cave, to see, with the mind's eye, the figures and actions which have generated the images on the wall of that cavern which is the stage.

Once the mind of the audience's member has accepted that shift of the drama, from the stage as a cavern wall, to the stage to be found within the imaginative, cognitive processes of the mind of the individual member of the audience, a performance of a work of Classical art has begun.

To bring this effect about, that by itself is not sufficient. Deductive solutions as such, do not exist in such matters. There must be passion. It is the musicality of the drama which supplies the indispensable medium of passion. For this purpose, the modern Classical stage must learn to sing. It must proceed from emphasis on the principles of Classical prosody. To achieve the effects of thorough-composition, it must condition its musicality through the influence of education in the art of Classical thorough-composition.

In such matters, what you think you are saying, and the manner in which you say it, may not agree. That should worry you. Therefore, you should refresh yourself, bathe your soul in Classical poetry and song, that your mind might become better attuned and habituated to communicating in that relatively well-performed mode which Classical art-forms exemplify for your guidance. On this account, there is a precious lesson to be learned by all citizens and other residents of the United States, especially those oppressed by the ruinous policy-trends of the past thirty-five years, from, among relevant other sources, the polished form of what is called the Negro Spiritual.

IN MEMORIAM

Tribute to Nina Ogden

by Alan Ogden

March 5—Our dear Nina slipped away February 28 at the age of 69. She grew up in the Bronx, New York City, the child of refugees from the Russian Civil War. Her first language was Russian. Her father worked in the needle trades and was an active union man in the International Ladies Garment Workers Union, and her mother was a union organizer. As a person is her parents' child, Nina's identity as a lifelong fighter for social justice was formed from the cauldron of the labor organizing battles of the 1930s, as was her patriotism and her lifelong, strong intellectual identity. Beginning as a pre-teen, she rode the New York subway alone to the Metropolitan Opera each Saturday afternoon, to see and hear live, and to learn, all the major operas. Her parents loved literature, especially Shakespeare, and studied Shakespeare to hone their English language skills, and Shakespeare was a central influence for Nina from that time to the present. Nina loved playing the violin and played at Carnegie Hall with a student orchestra. She graduated from Evander Childs High School in 1963 at the age of 16—the end of her schooling, but not the end of her education!

As a young girl, she joined the civil rights movement after talking to picketers she encountered on a New York street. One of them told her, "We are fighting for civil rights, and we won't stop until we've won." She joined the picket line—and the civil rights movement—on the spot, and when the picket line broke up, and somebody said it was time to go home, Nina's response was, "I thought we weren't stopping until we've won!" She was at the Washington March for Jobs and Freedom in 1963 ("I have a dream"), and the famous Selma-to-Montgomery March in 1965. Her 1960s civil

rights organizing even included hitchhiking across Canada to organize for Inuit rights with Stokely Carmichael.

I first met Nina in Fayetteville, Arkansas, in 1968. She was involved in a very hazardous effort by the textile workers to unionize the textile mills of that state, going to towns where being a union organizer was painting a target on your back.

We were married in Richmond, Virginia, in 1969. After the 1968 assassination of Dr. King, the civil rights movement was in a crisis, as the Black Panther Party and other black nationalists tried to assert intentions quite different from the intentions of Dr. King. Nina and I were told point blank that we were not wanted in the new version of the civil rights movement.

Nina worked in office jobs later, but in those early days, she worked in mill and factory jobs—in a cotton mill, at a book bindery, in a hat factory as a member of the Hat, Cap and Millinery Workers Union, and at Philip Morris as a member of the Tobacco Workers International Union.

August 1971 Wake-Up Call

We decided to put our political efforts into organizing the unemployed and the general community to support and back the union battles going on at the time, such as the strike by the workers of the *Richmond Times-Dispatch* newspaper. We called them Strike Support Committees, and had a little organization of nine close associates, who were like a little political committee to mobilize black churches, community organizations, peace groups, and others. When Dick Nixon announced his actions to end the Bretton Woods System and implement a national wage-price freeze in August

1971, we wanted to launch immediate mass organizing to oppose it, but we also realized our yawning ignorance of the issues involved, and of any coherent sense of economic policy.

So our little organization put two young women on a bus to New York City, with the mission of finding out who, among the vast tangle of purported social justice and leftist groups, could actually explain what was happening, and who intended to change it. Nina was one of those two delegates, and she phoned me up after a couple of days to say she had heard Lyndon LaRouche speak, and that he was the one we would be working with.

I strenuously and ignorantly objected, and continued to do so for several months. We had been well aware of LaRouche and his movement, and had been contacted by a labor organizer affiliated with LaRouche, but we had never been successfully recruited. So, as was so often the case over the years, Nina was right, and I was wrong, but Nina had no thought of giving up. We nine all went to New York for the national conference that Christmas, and after hearing Lyn speak and answer questions over the first day or two of the conference, I took Nina out for a walk on the cold wintry streets, and I told her, okay, I'm in. So (only because of Nina) we joined, not just as two recruits, but as a pre-formed nine-person local, the Hampton Roads Labor Committee, at the end of 1971.

God in Their Own Hearts

Nina, during these more than forty years in LaRouche's organization, has been a leader with a certain unique and fresh approach, always reaching out into new and unknown situations, talking to new and unknown people, looking for ways to touch the best in their natures. She was an initiator, a forward-driving force, who gave others confidence to discover a reflection of God in their own hearts, and—as they saw Nina herself do—to boldly act on that knowledge and that hope.

Her national and then international initiatives, on behalf of a new, just world system, involved a large array of political and diplomatic figures, including key figures dating back to the John F. Kennedy era, such as Jesuit Father Richard McSorley and Pierre Salinger; key church figures including Lebanese Maronite Catholic Bishop Elias El-Hayek, a central figure in the efforts to forge a lasting ecumenical peace in the Middle East; and including many of the major Twentieth Century giants in the FDR tradition of the Democratic Party, such as (just to name a few already publicly known), Sen. Eugene McCarthy, Sen. George McGovern, Congressman Jim Wright of Texas, and Congressman Andy Jacobs of Indiana. Precious, important people from Dr. King's movement became Nina's friends and political collaborators.

Nina made many organizing trips to the Great Plains states, and made a lasting impact especially in South Dakota and Nebraska, through personal, intensive, and open collaboration with leaders of the political world, of agriculture, Native American tribes, and others.

She volunteered to fight alongside the Irish for the cause of Irish liberty, to knock down the oppression and brutality of the British imperial system, right in its own back yard. After working with wonderful collaborators in Ireland, and after making a three-week organizing trip there in 2013, her unfinished work there included not only Irish national unity and independence from British governors and British decrees, but the revival of the plan, of Sinn Fein founder Arthur Griffith and independence leader Michael Collins, that Ireland might be established as a maritime industrial nation, harnessing its natural resources and taking its rightful place in the new, emerging world development geometry.

'Miracles Take Hard Work'

Close to Nina's heart was Mother Teresa, now officially known as Saint Teresa of Kolkata. Mother Teresa and Nina forged a close personal working relationship, to work to change the hearts of the nations to recognize the dignity of every individual human person. Nina believed that hearts can be changed and that good will triumph. Nina was able to forge a public collaboration between Lyndon LaRouche and Mother Teresa, the latter a person of key influence worldwide, especially on the crucial, central fight against the efforts of the Malthusians, who would rather eliminate billions of people than recognize the preciousness of the human soul.

Mother Teresa publicly authorized Nina Ogden of the Schiller Institute to issue 5,000 copies of a Schiller Institute broadsheet to be put into the hands of every delegate at the potentially very dangerous 1994 UN World Population Conference in Cairo, Egypt. It contained the text of Mother Teresa's address to the Presidential Prayer Breakfast in Washington, on the right and dignity of life.

Nina also solicited and organized a direct, very

public intervention by Mother Teresa against the death penalty for convicted murderer Joseph Roger O'Dell in Virginia, which even included a tape-recorded message in Mother Teresa's own voice, heard every half-hour on a Richmond radio news program, appealing to Gov. George Allen to spare O'Dell's life.

Mother Teresa once told Nina, "Most people think that miracles just happen, but you and I know that they take a lot of hard work." In a nutshell, this was Nina's guiding idea, and her assurance that if she gave people a lot of love, but no peace (also a Mother Teresa characteristic), that the good will triumph.

Nina and I were married for 48 years. I cherish every day I spent with her—now more than ever. I have abundant memories and graces because of her, that would fill to overflowing the biggest supertanker in the Suez Canal. She loved well, and I loved her in return. She was a singular, strong-willed, and wonderful woman.

Some of Nina's favorite lines were from *The Spiritual Canticle of St. John of the Cross*:

If, then, I am no longer seen on the
  common,
You will say that I am lost;
That, stricken by love,
I lost myself, and was found.

Nina is also survived by her son and daughter-in-law, Matthew and Meghan Ogden of Purcellville, Virginia; her daughter Erika Vaughan of Houston, Texas; her sister Lenore Sanders of Leesburg, Virginia; her nephew Joshua Smith of Harper's Ferry, West Virginia; and a host of in-laws and friends around the world.

A Selection of Articles by Nina

God Bless You, Mother Teresa
http://www.larouchepub.com/eiw/public/1997/eirv24n38-19970919/eirv24n38-19970919_058-god_bless_you_mother_teresa.pdf

Blessed Mother Teresa: A Fleeting Glimpse of the Sublime
http://www.larouchepub.com/eiw/public/2003/eirv30n42-20031031/eirv30n42-20031031_040-blessed_mother_teresa_a_fleeting.pdf

Eugene McCarthy: He Acted to Restore Our Nation's Purpose
http://larouchepub.com/eiw/public/2005/2005_50-52/2005_50-52/2005-52/pdf/34-35_50_nat_obit.pdf

Pierre Salinger and the Institution of the Presidency
http://www.larouchepub.com/eiw/public/2004/eirv31n42-20041029/eirv31n42-20041029_063-in_memoriam_pierre_salinger_and.pdf

A Westphalian Life: Msgr. Elias El-Hayek
http://www.larouchepub.com/eiw/public/2008/2008_20-29/2008_20-29/2008-22/pdf/64_3522.pdf

George McGovern: A Courageous Democrat in the Mold of JFK
http://larouchepub.com/eiw/public/2012/eirv39n42-20121026/_56_3942.pdf

www.ingramcontent.com/pod-product-compliance
Lightning Source LLC
Chambersburg PA
CBHW081604280526
45788CB00011B/3542